POETRY 101

STEVE LEONARD

Formatting by C. S. Cooper
www.cscooper.com.au

Illustrations by Garyl B. Araneta
www.fiverr.com/s/m5GZVwZ

Paperback ISBN: 978-1-7645144-0-8

Copyright © 2026 Steve Leonard
All rights reserved.

Contents

<u>Part A</u>	1
Gogglebox	3
Trousers	4
I've Got To Get My Hours Up	5
My Nose – Part 1	7
Undies	7
Magpie	8
Active Gear	9
Lemons	10
Trendy	11
Lockdown	12
Aisle 17	13
The Public Toilet App	15
The Futurist	16
There's A Spider In The Wing Mirror	18
There's A Cockroach In The Toaster	19
Woolies Christmas Eve 2020	20
Killing Time In Covid	22
The Three Little Pigs	25

Ben's Big Space Adventure	33
Freddy The Flathead	35
My Irish Skin	37
I'll Think I'll Be An Influencer	39
Lycraman	41
Porridge	44
The Post Office	45
Nowhere For Me To Hide	47
Mick The Jagger	49
Fishing	51
My Eyes Won't Open – 1959	55
Hot And Bothered	59
Year 9 Maths Lesson And The Hypnotist: 1970	61
A Day At The Seaside – 1962	65
Gosford Bank Visit – 1975	68
Trains 1976 – Strathfield To Parramatta	69
Bin Night	72
Trains: The Minister Speaks	74
Plumber Wants A Partner	76
Worms For Dinner	77
The Leg Cramp	79
Henry The Dog	80

Part B — 83

The Aussie Jesus	85
The Clash Of Two Kingdoms – Palm Sunday	87
My Last Christmas	89
I've Become Invisible	91
Luke 18:16-17	92
My Dad And The Cockroach	94
I Have This Sinking Feeling	96
Blackbird	97

My Nose – Part 2	98
Nursing Home Blues	99
Tribute To The Whistleblowers	100
The Marathon	102
My Feet	105
Funeral for a Friend	106
The Angel	108
Jock Martin	109
The Early Morning Walk – The Blue Mile	111
The Player	112
Musical Chairs	115
The Disrupter	116
The Morning Announcement	118
The Development Application – Mosman	120
The Digital Childhood	121
The Wonderful Age Of Silence	124
The Rant	126
Decolonisation	128
Character – Acts 10	130
"But What Have The Romans Ever Done For Us?"	132
I Wish I Was A Smart Phone	133
Toxic Town	134
Dads And Sons	135
Hostile Dog	136
"Proud sponsors of having a crack"	138
Profiling	139
Unpaired Words	140
I Want To Be A Bureaucrat	141
Vale Ann Marie Smith	143
The Resurrection Strategic Plan	144
The Good Bloke	147
The Quest For Chocolate Biscuits	149

PART A

Gogglebox

It's wonderous television
That we all enjoy to see
We watch a show called Gogglebox
On free to air TV

We're watching those who watch TV
It's such a great delight
They're sitting on their couch at home
They do this every night

We see their great reactions
To what they see on screen
Some laughter or disapproval
Occasionally a scream

But after a while I get restless
My attention starts to wane
I've reached a type of threshold
It's difficult to explain

So now I crave another fix
When I watch my nightly telly
I crave to watch those watching those
In a relationship of many

I anticipate the future
With just one remaining TV show
It could be Married At First Sight
I really don't quite know

It's low-cost entertainment
With everyone a star
We'll all become celebrities
From here to quite afar

With our half hour of exposure
Shown right across our nation
We'll be a nation of the famous
Deserving joyous adulation

And when we do our shopping
We'll stop and great each other
"I saw you on the telly
I watched it with my brother"

And we've been watched by someone else
And they in turn the same
And they've been seen in turn by those
The few that now remain

We'll have a camera in every home
And a microphone as well
We'll all crave to view each another
A synchronized type of hell

Everybody will have watched everybody!
We'll become a digital family
And it's all been through our widescreens
On Gogglebox TV.

2021

Trousers

The way that men wear trousers
change throughout the years
They start of way below the hip
but end up by their ears

It's fashionable to show undies
with baggy pants hung low
and it horrifies most mothers
Believe me I do know

With the crutch down near the kneecaps
with their undies quite exposed
it makes some movement tricky
but it's a style some young have chose

A bum-crack, to be honest,
Makes me fumble for small change,
To make a coin donation
Perhaps you think this strange?

But fear not 'cause waistbands alter
over decades if not years
and trousers creep up incrementally
up towards the ears

It happens oh so slowly
one centimetre at a time
like continents drifting slowly
in the years of sad decline

Yes, some older men are quite content
with pants around their chest
with a belt up near their armpits.
Such a 'comfy' way to dress!

2018

I've Got To Get My Hours Up

I've got to get my hours up!
It's all accreditation
whilst teaching all those fertile minds
the future of this nation

I've got to get my hours up!
I'm anxious and uptight
I've tossed and turned for hours now
and wasted half a night

I'VE GOT TO GET MY HOURS UP

I have my classification.
They say I'm quite 'proficient'
But if I don't get my hours up
I'll be judged as quite 'deficient'

I've got to get my hours up
or get the bleeding sack
I'll be shown the school-house front door
and I won't be coming back

Teaching once was easy
Just disengaged young minds
The angry and the docile
The usual sort you find

I am quite well qualified
from years way back in time.
But I need to get my hours up
and I'm running out of time!

Kids and parents love my classes
but they simply don't quite understand
I've got to get my hours up
Or get sadly left behind.

And then NESA lost some hours of mine
about a year ago
They're floating somewhere in cyberspace
But where I just don't know!

I'm usually slow to anger
and I'm normally not so bad
but having lost those precious hours,
it's left me more than mad

I've found an approved online course
though it looks a little dodgy
Something about 'continuums'

And harnessing 'power pedagogy'

But just to get my hours up
I'll knock it off quite quickly.
This jumping through the career hoops
can leave one feeling sickly

I've got to get my hours up
I hope I've made it clear!
I've got to get my hours up!
I just need another beer!

2018

My Nose – Part 1

A very useful implement
just slightly out of view.
When looking at it cross-eyed
it seems as if there's two.
With a gently sloping ski-field
and a view to either side.
It balances my glasses
and holds them to my eyes.
I'm glad it's not inverted
with problems ever coming
'cause an upturned nose
would surely cause some problems to my plumbing!

1994

Undies

My undies have lost their elastic,
no longer tight and close to my gut
They hang by the crutch of my trousers
and no longer snuggly to my butt

UNDIES

They were once so snug and supportive
A reason for joy every day.
So firm and so very uplifting
So comforting in every way
But the years and wear have been telling
Now threadbare and inclined to sag.
They're destined to be used for cleaning.
Or into a garbage bag!

2018

Magpie

There's a magpie in my garden.
He walks around a lot.
He catches lots of insects
and shows me what he's got

He swaggers up the driveway
with an insect in his beak.
He shows me what's for dinner.
He has no need to speak.

He's close by when I'm mowing
And should I disturb a moth or two,
he is quick to catch his quarry.
He knows exactly what to do

I love his haughty manner
and his upright cocky stance
and when he catches insects
I admire his little dance.

2018

Active Gear

I love to wear my active wear
I wear it round a lot.
I wear it when it's chilly.
I wear it when it's hot

I wear it when I go shopping.
And when I park the car
I park it next to the exit doors
So I don't have to walk too far

One size fits most figures
And it mostly comes in black
And yes I have my bulges
But I just gently push them back

I've tossed away the iron
it's such a waste of time.
This tightness of my clothing
Is absolutely fine

I get approving glances
when I power walk through the mall.
I'm on a serious fitness journey
They can see it one and all

Of course I could increase my daily exercise
and make this house quite clean
Perhaps help by using the vacuum cleaner
And squirt some Mister Sheen

I could exercise with my neighbours
Their names are John and Hetty
but they tend to be too serious
and I end up hot and sweaty

I'm flicking through the channels

whilst I watch a bit of telly
There's funerals that are now pre-paid
And cures for feet too smelly

There's ads for a fitness gadget
to shed weight without getting hot.
Electric toothbrush and new cleaners
I might just buy the lot!

I went shopping just the other day
And bought a 'high-vis' vest.
I wear it quite a lot these days
I might just toss away the rest.

2018

Lemons

My skin now smells of lemons
I'm somewhat embarrassed to say.
I noticed it whilst walking
down the hallway yesterday

When I turned around so quickly
I noticed a smell so faint,
The certain smell of lemons
refreshing and rather quaint

My wife now has in the bathroom
a bottle of this scent.
A squirt or two beforehand
before I make my sure descent

After weeks of this routine
and in the pores of my pale skin
the lemon has made great inroads.
It's well and truly in

It must be concentrated
and not diluted in any way
It's penetrated every inch of skin
I'm sorry to have to say

It's just a first-world problem,
that's what I tell my wife
about the workings of our toilet
and the complexities of life.

2018

Trendy

This pair of denim jeans
I bought them almost new
From an op-shop in the main street
Faded navy blue

I put them on the breakfast bar
And to make them look quite trendy
I cut them horizontally
Where both my legs are bendy

And now they look so trendy
At just a fraction of the price
I've saved myself a fortune
And I think they look quite nice

I get admiring glances
When I'm in the shopping mall
The look of recognition
From most, but not quite all

Some would like to argue
That it's an insult to the poor.
Yes, No, Maybe
I'm really not so sure

I had an egg for breakfast
Just the other day
So soft in the very centre
I like just that way

Some yolk went down my T-shirt
Cascading towards my belly
I thought that I should wipe it quick
Before it got too smelly

But then a new idea
So bold and rather 'chic'
Something original for the trendy?
Fake foodstains? Just the trick!

2018

Lockdown

The toilet roll stands proudly
So valued and very elevated
No longer just an after-thought
It's status perhaps belated

The shortage does remind us
Of our very basic needs
A topic not so conversed
But a warning we should heed

Are we so anal-retentive?
(It's a term now rarely heard)
We have an obsession with the toilet
Or is that too strong a word?

The present shopping frenzy
Of rolls in shopping trolleys
Desperation overload
Foolish human folly?

AISLE 17

We laugh at the panic buying
That we seek in other folk
As people do the rounds of shopping malls
We laugh like it's a joke

This virus has us thinking
Of the essentials in our life
I see the emergency items
When I go shopping with my wife

Beer and Coke-a-Cola
Hand Sanitizer as well
Rice and tinned processed meat
The stress begins to tell

One day it will be over
This lockdown will simply stop
And the toilet roll will be once again
Be barely thought of as we shop.

2019

Aisle 17

We are brawling over toilet paper
It's a silly tragic farce
It's just paper that we tend to use
When we want to clean ourselves

It was shown on all national news
Three women toe to toe
The screaming and obscenities
They put on quite a show

The police were called to sort it out
And bring a sense of order
To lower the heightened tension
For 2 women and a daughter

It rated rather high
I looked around the facility
With my observant little eye

There was a skid mark in the toilet bowl
It's age I couldn't tell
But in terms of general hygiene
It rated rather well

The ambience was noteworthy
Pleasant at least I thought
The lighting and the decor
The fittings not cheaply bought

Once I did the survey
I journeyed on my way
The survey all completed
I'd truly had my say

I've never been so consulted
To hear my point of view
My opinion so highly valued
All these surveys that I do!

2019

The Futurist

Today I saw a 'futurist'
Speaking on 'The Drum'
About how we now work well from home
And the trend for years to come

A historian studies history
Obtaining some degrees
Accumulating knowledge
And paying tuition fees

THE FUTURIST

So how do I become an expert
Of what one day will come
So I can speak with authority
On the ABC nightly Drum?

Do I enrol at university
And study Tea Leaves 101
And learn to read a crystal ball
So not to get it wrong

Do I study correlation
And learn to crunch the data?
Or is it actual causation
Is that what I'm really after?

As for margin of error
If I get it completely wrong
I can just simply shrug my shoulders
And pivot to a different song

I think I'll stick with history
Of which I know I'm certain
Of revolutions and social change
I do recall the Iron Curtain

I cannot see a career path
As a futuristic type
The predictions and observations
The jargon and the hype

Covid 19 is a test for our fair country
And I write in isolation
Perhaps I'm bored or in need of work
Or some better inspiration!

2020

There's A Spider In The Wing Mirror

There's a spider in my wing mirror
There's one on the other side as well
I don't know if they're acquainted
It's rather hard to tell

They're catching insects at a 100km per hour
As I drive at quite a speed
It gives them a source of daily food
Upon which I guess they feed

Do they meet each night on my windscreen
And have a little chat?
Do they discuss their family problems
And where the world is at?

How did they take up occupancy
On my lovely aging car?
How did they find their present abode
Did they travel from afar?

Did one throw itself at a spinning wheel?
And then hung on for dear life
Then pulled on board his several children
Before saving his dear wife

Did they then climb up towards the mirror
And overcome a sense of dizzy
As the wheel spun in rapid rotation
Was their hair all wild and frizzy?

Or did they jump from a branch overhanging
And landed upon the car
And then find their way to the mirror
It's really not that very far?

Do they look into the mirror?

With eight eyes wide apart
Do they get a fright when they see themselves
Palpations to the heart?

Do they enjoy the freedom of the highway
With the wind blowing through their hair
The exhilaration of the journey
Without any trouble or a care?

Should I get the tin of Mortein
And end their heroic life?
And spray in the direction?
It would certainly please my wife!

2021

There's A Cockroach In The Toaster

There's a cockroach in the toaster
I'm pretty sure it's true
There's tell-tale signs to show it's there
I'm talking about its poo

There's always crumbs to feed on
It leads a happy life
But I can tell you it is not welcome
Especially by my wife

I suspect it's most unpleasant
When at breakfast we apply the heat
He must be cooking deep inside
But it won't accept defeat

It's really hard to dislodge it
I give it my best shot
I shake the toaster upside down
I give it all I've got

But there's so many little crevices
For a cockroach to live and hide
I've done my best to get rid of it
You can't say I haven't tried

I admire this little critter
Who gets roasted every morning
He toughs it out, and without a doubt
I'd say it is his calling!

2020

Woolies Christmas Eve 2020

It's Christmas Eve and we're shopping
We've been queued for quite a while
We came for last minutes items
We've been down several aisles

We have some festive spirit
We are both in a pretty good mood
There's no point being miserable
Or being short or rather rude

The lady just in front of us
Has a bag that says Happy Easter
"You're just a couple of weeks ahead of yourself"
I tell her just to tease her

We are close to the actual checkout
Magazines are on display
It's all about the younger royalty whose
stories refuse to go away

So Kate and Will are planning a rescue
For Harry they are concerned
After a marriage to his Meghan
And with his family feeling spurned

Another tells a story
of a royalty telling lies
And of spreading nasty rumours
To wreck their privileged lives

Another member of the royalty
who is cruel beyond belief
Sometimes saintly but now so clearly
Is the villain causing grief

The Queen is now most upset
'Palace sources' say she's grieving
Andrew is languishing on the outer fringe
And with Meghan and Harry leaving

The lady at check-out
Has a special Christmas top
She goes about her business
She's fast and doesn't stop

She seems to be in good sprits
Though the pace is a little frantic
I decide to add to the festive air
With a silly little antic

She puts items in the green grocery bag
And hesitates to add 1 more
She doesn't want to make it heavy
Or see us struggle out the door

My wife says 'add the item anyway'
I said 'its ok" with festive cheer.
"My wife can carry the heavy bags
That's why I brought her here!"

So, I groan as I lift the 3rd bag
I'm laying it on quite thick.
I make out I have real back pain

I try to sound quite sick

"It's the Leafy-Mix!" I tell her
"It does it every time!"
I groan and wear a grimace
"Don't worry, I'll be fine"

She laughs at my silly antics
She enjoys this brief respite
She shares her Christmas spirit
It's almost Christmas night

And as we head towards the carpark
We laugh…we've had our fun
A bit of Christmas frivolity.
Yes, Christmas time has come.

2020

Killing Time In Covid

Part 1

I'm killing time in Covid.
I've a list of things to do
I wouldn't normally do them
I have to say it's true

It's the saddest of expressions
To say 'killing time' at all
When I think of this expression
I'm usually quite appalled

Because our days are certainly numbered
We know this to be true
To be killing time in any way
Is a monstrous thing to do

KILLING TIME IN COVID

Killing time by the hour
With an eye upon the clock
Oh great! it's almost dinner time
The killing can now stop

Dinner time brings respite
From this genocide of time
I'm putting on some extra kilos
Now, there's a certain crime

I ventured into the garage
I was feeling rather strange
I decided to do a clean out
Or at least a major re-arrange

The nails and screws are now sorted
As well as lots of fiddly things
I've filled them "Miscellaneous"
With a collection of some springs

The sockets have been sorted
According to their size
And then according to their brand-name
Much to my wife's surprise

I'm not so normally tidy
It's not my usual way
But this lockdown has quiet changed me
Will this transformation stay?

The cutting blades now stand together
Upright and at attention
Last month I couldn't find one
I confess and have to mention

The glues in one container
The sticky tapes as well
My son approves of this new order

From his expression I can tell

All spanners are in the tool-box
With the screw-drivers close beside
I've never seen so much order
Almost tears in both my eyes

This killing time has benefits
I think it's been worthwhile
The workbench looks resplendent
I must display those files

I've tossed some crap into the wheely bins
A real purging of the mess
This cleansing of my inner-self
To which I publicly now confess.

Part 2

Then's there's the banes of my existence
Two warts that had escaped my eye
I decided to remove them
Or at least have a decent try

The first was on my right foot
Just down from the third toe
It has always been hard to get at
Because it's located on the sole

The other on my cheek bone
Perhaps 4 or 5 years old
It should have had it treated long ago
If truth be honestly told

I found the ointment in the bathroom
In the draw that holds my mess
It really needs a clean out
More killing time, I guess

So, I've burnt the offending tissue
With the ointment I applied
And I've managed to dodge the blindness
From getting ointment in the eye

I'm happy with all these outcomes
In a Covid sort of way
This attention to what was minor
In my pre-lived Covid days.

2021

The Three Little Pigs

(The true story of Morris, Boris and Doris)

You've heard the story when you were about three
of the 3 Little Pigs when you sat on a knee
Of your mother or father who told you this tale
Of the pigs who built houses and of two that did fail

A wolf was the baddy who did want to eat
The three little pigs because of their meat
He was keen for some pork because of his hunger
He liked pigs of all types but especially the younger

In the tale that you heard the pigs won in the end
Because the wolf climbed on a roof and began to descend
Down a chimney of a house that was made out of bricks
After blowing down the two made of straw and of sticks

But is that the truth? Is the truth easy to see?
Were the pigs simply foolish at least two out of three.
I think it's time now to be quite honest with you
You deserve to be told what is actually true

The pigs spent all day just watching TV.

They watched Grand Designs - not surprising to me.
They became house building know-alls – they debated all day.
Not once leaving a chair. They had too much to say!

They started wearing safety gear -they really looked the part
With brightly coloured safety hats, to easily tell them apart
With fluro vests and low-slung belts sitting snugly on their hips
With sun protection block out and cream on their lips

The house was like a construction site – it really was a mess
Tools left lying around and now I must confess
Mum's nerves were becoming a little frayed – and noticeably upset
She was worried she might just explode with words she might regret

"Go out and build! It's now time for action!"
She looked at their faces to get their reaction.
"Build some houses and get on the telly.
Become famous as builders and known well by many!"

Still young and quite silly and with the confidence of fools
With little to carry and just a few tools
When the clock struck 9 they went on their way
Mum called "goodbye" as she gave them a wave

At least two of the pigs were apparently clueless
Lazy as well and obviously foolish.
A home built out of straw deserves outright contempt!
Even if it was their first modest attempt

They were happy enough and filled with false pride
Morris, Boris and Doris all entered inside.

THE THREE LITTLE PIGS

"Let's all just relax. The job was quite easy!"
(There were gaps in the wall and the draughts were quite breezy)

But young Boris the pig had a problem. His problem was wind
He tried to contain the force from within
And during the night he completely let rip
It was of such power that he strained both his hips

The house then collapsed and fell down around them
"Boris, you human!" said his siblings astounded.
"You've wrecked this fine home. You've left it in tatters!
Re-build now we must. It's the one thing that matters!"

Brother Morris it must be honestly said
was a thick as the other...in terms of his head.
"We'll rebuild with some sticks. I'm sure they're much stronger."
They're free, and admit, it won't take much longer"

And so, the next day they went gathering some sticks
From a wood up the road, past old farmer Hicks.
They made holes in the ground and shoved the sticks in
"This house will be fine," young Morris did grin

Home number two was built in less than a day
With a door and a window and a view of a bay
They slept on the floor. They were so tired that night
But at 2 in the morning, they awoke with a fright

There was rain and some hail. The rain leaked through the roof
The pigs huddled together, no longer so aloof.
"This house is a failure!" said Doris their sister.
"From now I'm in charge!" (They could hardly resist her)

And Doris the sister was true to her word
She called a meeting next morning and she made her

views heard

"It's bricks, you two ninnies. It's bricks that we need
I'll give you advice. You'd do well to take heed"

"From now on I'm in charge of the likes of you two
And you'll do as I say. There's a lot we must do
We have no money to speak of, but we must find some bricks
We'll use cunning and guile and 1 or 2 tricks"

In no time at all Doris spoke of her plan.
It was agreed that they needed a truck or a van
A truck stop was just 10 minutes away.
It's where two of them waited the very next day

A large truck soon pulled in. It was carrying bricks
The driver went for a meal in the café called "Nick's"
He ordered a juicy bacon/egg roll. They watched while he ate
"Those bricks will be ours. There's no time to wait!"

Doris soon picked the lock of the driver's truck door.
Boris crouched down below quite close to the floor
Doris short-wired the ignition. The engine soon started
Quite soon into gear and they quickly departed

With Doris in charge of steering and Boris the clutch
To the truckie they yelled "we thank you so much"
With his mouth now wide open and with grease on his chin
He seemed totally unable to take it all in

Morris was waiting just over the hill
He'd made a clearing of sorts and the truck drove straight in
Morris placed branches to conceal the large truck
The pigs had trouble believing their luck

With high fives all around the pigs were delighted

THE THREE LITTLE PIGS

Doris and Boris from the truck they alighted.
"I'm proud of you both," Doris said to her brothers
"As would our father and as would our mother"

The bricks were unloaded. They were heavy it's true.
They worked long after midnight. It was closer to 2
When they slept in the field for a number of hours.
They slept like angels amongst the grass and the flowers

Next day they stole other needed building supplies
Not once were they captured. It's had to know why.
A Bunnings store they stole from. They emptied the shelves
The crime-spree continued. They were as quiet as elves

Whilst the brothers cleared trees following Doris's instructions.
Doris looked at Youtube for the tips on construction.
"It's not that hard. Just one brick at a time!
Our house will be built from the proceeds of crime"

It less than one month the house was quite done
It was hard work for sure but also quite fun
A bedroom for each with an en-suite as well
The brothers agreed that the house looked quite swell

The rooms were quite spacious. There was a sauna and spa
"We will welcome our family and friends from afar
Pigs will be welcome. We will welcome our kind
But never the humans who eat bacon and rind"

But as you know most criminals are caught
This is a lesson for sure and deserves to be taught
A detective Inspector was given a file
His name was De-Wolf. He was known for his guile

De-Wolf had been in charge of dis-organised crime
He knew he'd succeed if given fair time

THE THREE LITTLE PIGS

His record was great. He was a master detective
Every criminal has flaws with plans quite defective

He looked for good clues. He checked CCTV
After watching for days. He was astounded to see
A pig driving a truck! It was carrying a load
Of thousands of bricks as it sped up the road

He figured it would take a number of pigs
To handle the job of driving a rig
Posters were made with a reward for information
To help capture the master thieves of the nation

Newspapers, TV and public assisted
The thieves would be caught. De-Wolf quite insisted.
In their palatial home the pigs were bemused
"They'll never catch us," Doris enthused

"Our friends in high places will save all our bacon.
At least I hope so with the money they're makin.
Protection isn't cheap and we've paid lots of money
The efforts of police are futile and funny"

It's true that the pigs' empire had grown
They had corrupted in high places if the truth could be known
Land deals, casinos and in the EPL
A club so successful and known equally well

Doris was mastermind and quite without peer
She snacked on caviar and sipped from a beer.
"De-Wolf will never ever get us to court
The judges I tell you have been carefully bought"

So how does it end this fanciful tale?
Should I be honest with you? Will truth prevail?
More than one ending? Perhaps at least two?
The ending you read will depend upon you

THE THREE LITTLE PIGS

1st Ending

De-Wolf the Inspector was patient to secure
Convictions for stealing, for fraud and what's more
He never doubted that he would succeed in the end
And a long time in prison the three pigs would spend

He reviewed all the evidence. He never lost patience.
He bugged all their homes and used some surveillance.
With the 3 pigs actually flaunting their wealth
He vowed to arrest them by hard work and stealth

And so in a brilliantly co-ordinated raid
On a warehouse, their home and a luxury yacht was made
Helicopters, speed boats and abseiling police
In locations in Britain, Paris and Nice

Whilst good people slept contently in bed
The three little pigs were solemnly lead
To three cells in prison in the middle of night
De-Wolf could hardly contain his delight

And though the 3 pigs in court pleaded together not-guilty
The jury convicted all three quite quickly
"We've been framed by the police!" Doris protested.
It was heard in the courtroom so small and congested

Prison life is inconvenient. The pigs do agree
But not permanent at all; just temporary
They think of the good days with a smile on their face
And yes Doris has plans to get then out of this place

2nd Ending

You'll agree little pigs can be decidedly cute
Not like a wolf who is a bit of a brute
Perhaps with the pigs your sympathy resides
In spite of their crime, in spite of their lies

No-one has been hurt, injured or made lame
Yes their thievery and stealing is a bit of a shame
But this is a win for the pigs in world full of humans
The 'underdog' victorious with the police certainly fuming

Accusations are made and rumours abound
Reputational mud is thrown around
Some of it sticks on the little pigs' skin
But they're happy in mud. For them it's a win

De-Wolf finally accepts after years on the case
That his efforts have failed. It hurts to lose face
But with a pension of sorts in a nice comfy home
It too made of bricks. He lives not alone

He is convinced of the guilt of the 3 little pigs
But he admires in a way the way that they live
From humble beginnings they have made a fine life
He heard that young Boris has actually found a nice wife

Doris has formed a political party
And Morris assists her. Yes, she is the smarty
Quite respectable all three pigs are now content
To live the good life, though not heavenly sent

And so, we come to the end of this tale
Of the three little pigs and two houses that failed
The third house of bricks still looks splendid today
We toast their success and say Hip Pip Hooray!

2021

Ben's Big Space Adventure

Ben was bored. It was just 10 o'clock.
He poked with his toe at the hole in his sock

He looked at the task for the lesson that day.
If only Google Classroom would just go away

He asked politely if he could be excused.
"To take a leak," was the term that he used

He wandered out and went on his way
The teacher was sweet; just there for the day

He walked around and looked at the view
To the oval he went with nothing to do

The sun was warm. He had thoughts on his mind
But it wasn't the task that he had just left behind

Oval 4 was where he now was headed
The grass just cut, just recently shredded

He kicked at the grass and got grass on his shoes
He felt so at peace..no sign of the blues

From a window nearby in room M206
A teacher was watching and rather transfixed

"What's Ben up to? Wait till I see him!
Compass chronicle for his absenteeism"

But then in an instant young Ben disappeared
In a split of a second; so hard to believe

The Science teacher watching was left in no doubt.
"It's a pesky Black Hole! There's a few round-about"

His parents were called. It was hard to explain
The principal perplexed and feeling the strain

"Sorry Mrs M...... Don't be alarmed!
We have no reason yet, to think that Ben's harmed

I'm sure he'll turn up in an hour or two
He's just travelling through space and enjoying the view"

Ben's mother replied "He's nothing but trouble!
He's away with the fairies! He lives in a bubble!

When he gets back, I'll have something to say
For making us worried and going away!"

The ovals were closed. The decision was made
Some kids were not happy. They whined and complained

As for Ben? He travelled happily afar
Galaxies, planets, and millions of stars

It was the trip of a lifetime. Such a smile on his face
"It's better than schoolwork. This travelling in space!"

He went through a wormhole. It was risky but fun
Then ended up roughly where the journey begun

He had travelled for decades, or so Ben did think
But he landed in Earth and had reason to blink

His watch showed he been gone less than a day
"Time travel is confusing, that's all I can say,"

Ben went to the classroom for the 6th period that day
He was sent to the principal. Not surprising you say

"Now listen young Ben. You take this nice card
You're now on a level. You might think I'm quite hard

But we can't have kids taking off into space
Imagine the media all over the place!"

"It's those pesky Black Holes, sir. And through your window I see your car's just vanished from under that tree."

2023

Freddy The Flathead

It was a lovely Monday morning.
Freddie was just loving life.
An early swim before breakfast
Not a worrying thought in sight

He saw Sammy in the distance.
"What a morning Sammy my mate?"
Sammy the snapper called back to him.
"Absolutely 1st rate!"

Freddie was feeling peckish.
His eyes darting left and right
He caught a glimpse of a tasty prawn.
Such heavenly delight!

Freddie didn't see the fishing line.
Or the hook inside the prawn
He opened up his jawbone
As having a great big yawn

He didn't see the man and his children.
Fishing from the tinny
A nice young girl had caught him
She was tall and rather skinny

He was pulled towards the small boat
He struggled to get free.
But the strength of the girl was too much for him,
As Sammy could clearly see

Freddie was yanked right out the water
And held in the father's grip

The hook was pulled from the side of his mouth
And right through his upper lip

He heard the dad's voice say, "Too small!"
Then Freddie was flying through the air
"If a Pelican sees me, I'm done for
Freddie was close to despair

Sammy watched from a short distance.
The splash was loud and clear.
"Are you alright my friend Freddie?
You're injured, I do fear"

Freddie's face looked misshapen.
He was feeling out of wack
His face was bulging on the left side.
His tongue poking through a crack

"The bugger threw back in the water!
I've a hole in my left cheek.
I have to plug the hole with the tip of my tongue,
And that's why it's hard to speak"

"And I have to spit out water
Every few seconds or so.
I wish he'd thrown me in the bucket
The useless so and so!"

"If get snagged on my other cheek,
With a hole on either side,
I'll be spitting out water at a rate of knots
I might as well be fried!

This 'catch and release' is a nightmare,
For the likes of you and me.
They think they are being so kind to us
They don't see the tragedy

I was hoping to father millions
In the warmer months ahead
Which girl is going to look at me nicely now
When they see the state of me head!"

Sammy was determined
to offer a different point of view.
To offer an honest perspective
Of what humans fail to do

"As if the bloke who released you
could manage swimming underwater,
With holes in both sides of his mouth
And whilst talking to his daughter!

"Come on, let's go swimming.
And swim the blues away
The water's warm and the sun is shining.
Let's not waste a single day."

2023

My Irish Skin

My Irish skin is now paper thin.
It really is an issue
It simply isn't like its former self.
Now more like paper tissue

If I bump a branch or a little twig
When trimming a garden tree
A purple blotch will just appear.
It's so annoying me

I see the good doc twice a year.
He tells me to take more care
He freezes off some BCC's
From the head amongst my hair

MY IRISH SKIN

My wife was born in Italy
She has superior skin.
I'm sometimes mistaken as her dad!
It's hard to take this in

What's the point of having wit.
And lots of Irish charm
When your skin is quite decrepit
especially on the arms

And a high IQ has lost its gloss
When I see my sad reflection.
I see the cost of each passing year
With a simple skin inspection

I check all the Aldi catalogues.
I look for a new skin kit
I'm surprised I haven't found one yet
I'm sure it'd be a hit

Just buy the kit and take it home
And peel off a nice new layer
Glue it on in some simple way
On my face from ear to ear

Cut some holes for my eyes and mouth.
And a section for my nose
No need to worry about my skin
On my feet or on my toes

And then of course on my arms and hands
The bits that see the sun
The whole job done in just a couple of hours.
And then I could have some fun

I think I'll go for a darker skin,
With a subtle olive glow
A hint of Mediterranean

You understand, I know

In the meantime, I'll keep my eye out.
For replacement Aldi skin
When the job is done, my skin will no longer be,
Paper tissue thin.

I'll Think I'll Be An Influencer

I'm getting closer to retirement
I've just turned 69.
I'm running out of gas, I think
I'm running out of time

And I struggle with the little things,
In deciding what to do
What socks to wear each morning,
What colour, brown or blue?

Do I wear my shirt in or out?
Should I give the car a wash?
Should I have toast for brekky this morning?
Are my teeth in need of floss?

I want to work more from home. I think
It's the modern thing to do
Connect through social media
Perhaps a dream come true?

I have heard the term 'influencer.'
I can hardly believe it's true.
I heard it's very lucrative
For the little that they do

It would have to be a piece of cake,
If what they say is true
Getting paid for advising others,
Exactly what to do

I'LL THINK I'LL BE AN INFLUENCER

If course, I'd need a platform
(No, it's nothing to do with trains)
It's on the net (not the fishing type.
(Believe me, not the same)

I hear TikTok is now popular
(And I don't mean clocks upon a wall)
It's that social media type of thing.
Now taking the world by storm

I'd need help with the tech set-up,
Just hours, not days or weeks
Before giving blokes about my age
the guidance that they seek

Tell them about car tyres
And who to buy them from
And if they shop for mouse traps
Get them cheap but also strong

Advice on stain removal
Tablets for that boost
I'd do a little bit of research.
Both on tonics and on juice

I might need to smarten up a bit,
And use that anti-wrinkle cream.
There are things I simply have to do
For this brilliant little scheme

And it appears that some self-adoration.
Is needed for success
I confess it will seem very strange to me
To obsess with how I dress

But then the money starts rolling into
My little bank account
(Not sure how this really works

Or even the exact amount!)

You see, if 20-year-olds can make a living,
With the little that they know
I'd make an absolute killing,
From this 'influencer' show

I'll be rich and rather famous!
Success without the sweat.
No grunt or sustained effort
Just money, and no regret.

2024.

Lycraman

My doctor looked quite puzzled.
He frowned and scratched his chin.
"After your latest fitness surge
You should be fit and rather thin"

"Well, I cycle every morning
I go up and down some hills
I thought if I kept this up,
I could rid myself of pills"

I sometimes have a morning off
But I didn't tell him that
I'm still soft around the middle
But I wouldn't say I'm fat

I'm watching what I'm eating
Well, it's true I do most days.
I like a biscuit with my cup of tea
With my cup of hot Earl Gray

I'm mostly honest with my doctor
There's good will and also trust

LYCRAMAN

I sometimes tell a little white lie,
But only if I must.

He was looking quite defeated.
He was now clutching at some straws
He then asked me when I'm cycling,
Exactly what it was I wore

I told him that I wore some old shorts,
With a T-shirt that's quite baggy
With joggers or thongs upon my feet
(I admit I look quite daggy)

"That's it! You should be wearing lycra!
When you have your morning ride
It'll make the world of difference
Now let me tell you why

You'll melt away the kilos,
If you wear the lycra gear
It's generally available
And not particularly dear

It does 'things' to your metabolism
I guarantee it's true
You'll be doing proper exercise
It'll change the shape of you."

I promised him I'd buy some
I went shopping straight away
I quickly bought some lycra gear.
(Not cheap, I'd have to say)

I stood in front of the mirror
I turned this way and that
There were some bulges in some places
And mostly caused by fat

LYCRAMAN

I wore it proudly the next day
I was keen to look the part
I cycled away on my ancient bike
It was an early morning start

I got nods and smiles and winks that day
From other lyrca wearers
(I was now a valued member
But not yet an office bearer.)

I was no longer Mr Invisible,
Amongst the exercise elite
I was now totally accepted
From my head down to my feet.

But if you go to Europe's cities
Where they ride around a lot
Cycling is a form of transport.
Whether it's cold or very hot

Men on ladies bikes each morning.
In suits and shirt and ties
With a basket on the handlebars.
No-one laughs or asks them why

The next day I took my lyrca gear
To the local charity shop
"You can have this lot I told them."
They told me, "thanks a lot"

It was really quite cathartic
To get rid of all the gear
I felt a burden had been lifted
I felt a certain amount of cheer

Yes, I'm generally quite ignored.
By the lyrca wearing mob
As I cycle in my baggy T shirt

That I confess, I like a lot!

2024

Porridge

It's the breakfast food of champions
It's famous throughout the world
A breakfast bowl of porridge
What is say is not absurd

It's quick to cook and tasty
Have it hot or have it cold
Rich or poor doesn't matter
Nor if you're very young or old

But don't let it set like concrete
In the bowl if you should delay
Then you'll need a chisel and a hammer
Hard work for half a day!

Porridge will keep you regular!
(We all know what that means
It will flush out well your insides
And leave them superbly clean)

So, get down to the local porridge shop
And buy a bowl or two
Forget the Golden Arches
And the muck they serve to you

So many stars upon the big screen
Athletes and singers too
Swifties by the millions
I kid you not. It's true!

They love their bowl of porridge!
And it's true, I have to say

When it comes to the morning breakfast
It's porridge every day!

2024.

The Post Office

It used to be so easy,
At the local Post Office Shop
You buy a stamp and stick it on
And then out the door you'd pop

A card to send overseas,
For a birthday or celebration
New Zealand is not so far away,
They're our neighbours as a nation

So, imagine the bemusement of my wife,
When she went to the Post Office shop
She had a card in an envelope,
Needing a stamp to stick on top

The man looked very pleasant,
On the other side of the screen
A simple job for him you'd think,
From what we've previously seen

"I'm not used to selling postage stamps,
And in dealing with the mail"
And whilst my wife was a little surprised
She was sure he would prevail

He went straight onto his computer
He looked perplexed to say the least
He shifted his weight from foot to foot
He seemed particularly ill of ease

My wife ever helpful, gave him a suggestion

THE POST OFFICE

"Perhaps weigh the card and envelope?"
She thought it helpful just to mention
She wasn't trying to embarrass him,
I can vouch for her intention

"And it might just need an extra stamp,
Depending on how much it weighs"
It didn't seem to help him much
He stood immobilised and dazed

Another worker then appeared,
And provided him assistance,
Within another minute or two they worked it out
Success from their persistence

I had been waiting near the door
I went with wife that day
I decided to come in and investigate,
The cause for her delay

I'd finished checking out the air-fryers
And knives and mobile phones
Self-help books for the young and old
A book on precious stones

It's great that the good old Post Office
Still sells a stamp or two
That the staff can still help with your mail
And work out what to do

We walked down the street to the carpark
And it's true we were both amused
At the simple task of sending mail
Or were we just bemused?

2024

Nowhere For Me To Hide

Confession of a seven-year-old

(dedicated to my migrant hostel friend Patrick Tiernan 1)

For me it was just playground fun
Just an innocent fantasy.
To be running around like a knight of old
Full of virtuous ecstasy

Dragons to kill and rescue plots
To free a damsel from a prison cell
And kill her tormentors one by one
And to curse loudly as they as they fell

And whilst my school friends played games of their own
My imagination knew no limits to roam
Mountain tops and fast flowing streams
Over the asphalt with my vivid dream

But after while it was not enough
I needed a prisoner and one not too tough
I spied a boy, a fellow classmate
A scrawny lad – no need to hesitate

I grabbed him and said, "you come with me
You are my prisoner as you can see
Stand over here whilst I am away
Remain right here and do not stray"

He protested as prisoners are inclined to do
"I do not want to play with you!"
I ignored his protests – they were rather weak
And marched him over my castle keep

I left him there and warned him to stay
And returned to battle a short distance away
I returned to his cell and to my surprise

It was empty according to my startled eyes

Patrick was gone. How dare he stray!
And wander off and so far away.
He had escaped with ease and what is more
His defiance shook me to the core!

I found and grabbed him and dragged him back
He came unwillingly like a reluctant sack
I showed no mercy (between me and you)
He was a rather distressed. It was certainly true

The bell then rang, and the game then ended
My medieval adventure now quite suspended
That night I gave little thought to Patrick's plight
And slept quite soundly throughout the night

But the very next day whilst seated in class
On those hard wooden seats so hard on the bottom
Patrick's mum appeared with Patrick as well
She was pointing at me I could easily tell

She looked at me with accusing eyes
Her parental anger not one bit disguised
I felt rather ashamed. My remorse sincere
I confess to you now, my audience here

But fate has many twists and turns
And within months my world had completed turned
Off to Australia to start a new life!
To leave behind my trouble and my strife

We moved to a place called New South Wales
So far from England and my troubled tales
Surely my past was safely behind me
A fresh start in this amazing country

I heard a whistle just outside the door

There are kids around here and what is more
There'll be someone to play with perhaps boys like me
There's fun to be had just wait and see!

I watched the whistler walk away down a path
He was making his way to the communal bath
The dread of familiar recognition
Super-hyped brain cognition!

He ears stuck out from the side of his head
Just like Patrick's if the truth is to be said
But how could this be? It must be a dream
Deep inside myself an impulse to scream

And Patrick it was. In Australia like me
His whole family was here I could easily see
They were living near us…almost next door
I wanted to disappear in a hole in the floor!

My infamy had followed me from England to here
There was nowhere to hide. It was abundantly clear
God was determined I wouldn't easily escape
The sins from my past. You could call it fate

The world is so small. I learned whilst quite young
With no chance of escaping when you've done something wrong.

2024

Mick The Jagger

So old rocker Mick got engaged
Some people consider him aged
He's now in his 8th decade
And while some are concerned
For others it's simply outrage

MICK THE JAGGER

The lady in question I should tell
Is an American dancer named Mel
Perhaps number 9 child?
Is it crazy or wild?
The passage of time will soon tell

Old Mick still sports slender hips
And still enhanced when it comes to his lips
Does he have implants or dentures?
And in restaurants I gather
He's quite generous when it comes to a tip

Is Mick's personality simply out of this world
Or is it his money that attracts all the girls?
He still sings a good song
With the band going strong
Why judge that it's rather absurd?

Most 80-year-old men are very sedate
And in recliners they wait for their eventual fate
Perhaps in palliative care
And with little or no hair
With an eye on the heavenly gate

So, Mick's slightly ahead of his game
Science allows some men who wish to remain
In perpetual youth
It seems to be true.
Jonathon Swift would say it's a shame

From Mick, I'm just a decade away
Will young women one day come my way?
I have limited means
Just a spare $1000 it seems
And no risk of going astray.

2025

Fishing

Patrick again...part 2

Patrick and his older brother David invited young me
To go fishing the next day to a spot near the sea
Off to the harbour at Port Kembla by bus
With my new fishing rod that I loved very much

We walked down a jetty and found a good gap
Organised our gear and had a quick snack
Swimming down near the pylons, the fish were so many
"Let's get into it now," said Patrick to Lenny

It was a large school of Yellow Tail and they took to our bait
We pulled in one after another with hardly a wait
For a number of hours; for most of the day
The fish kept on coming I'm delighted to say

I decided to take my fine bounty home
To help feed my family with fish off the bone
My mum would fry them in her new electric pan
She'd be so proud of her fine little man

I needed a box or bag or a bucket at least
To carry them home for our very fine feast
I saw an old leather bag with a clasp on the top
A little dusty and dirty but fine for the job

Patrick and David had a catch of their own
And with enough fish for us all to take home
By late afternoon we decided to leave
With our bounty so big it was hard to believe

I entered our hut quite bursting with pride
You should have seen the look on my own mother's eyes
"I've got fish for our dinner. There's enough for us all!"

FISHING

It wasn't a hero's return I clearly recall

The reaction of mum was not what I expected
The stink from the fish her nose now detected
"Get those stinky fish out of here!
Into the rubbish. Have I made myself clear?"

Resigned and deflated, I walked to the bin
I had learnt that some days you simply can't win
I had to walk past the communal amenity hut
Of showers and toilets. The doors were shut

I heard a woman singing; probably having a bath
I heard the splashing of water as I stood on the path
A small window was open about 6 feet up high
Just over the bath and quite close to the sky

Wouldn't it be funny I thought to myself
If when having a bath alone by oneself
Some fish came from heaven and arrived with a splash
And floated around whilst you're having a bath

To bathe in a bath surround be fish
It wouldn't be everyone's natural wish
But it would just be joke and a laugh and a giggle
(The fish now dead had lost all their wriggle)

A voice said "Stephen don't play with fire.
Just go to the bin. You know mum's desire
Get rid of the fish. Just do as you're told
Unless you want to die quite young and not very old"

I convinced myself the window was too high
It seemed far above me away in the sky
I would probably miss even with aim
And If I missed quite completely there would be no chance of blame

I bent down into the bag and with fingers clasped

together
Scooped about a dozen of the fish. They were as light as a feather
I looked up to the window and decided to try
Although just a metre or so the window seemed high

And would you believe what happened that day?
It seemed the fish were sucked in through the window in a peculiar way.
A moment of silence, of quiet repose
Then a scream of the ages. My blood nearly froze!

It gave me a fright I panicked right there
So straight to the bin without a second to spare
Into the bin went the fish and the bag
(Except for the fish that I no longer had)

I scurried back to our hut and closed the door tight
I waited in fear throughout most of the night
Imagine how upset my parents and understandably mad
If they learned that their son was so foolish and bad

Days past and then weeks I heard not a sound
No mention of fish in a bath. No rumours abound
Life went back to normal whatever normal means
For an eight year old boy who lived in his dreams

2018

Many decades later after the funeral of John
Over a good cup of tea quite hot and quite strong
We chatted with his wife Vera for an hour or two
United in grief and as friends want to do

Vera, my mum's best friend from the old hostel days
Looked at me with fondness and then with a faraway gaze
She spoke of great times on the hostel and the making of friends

Friendships forever. Sustained to the end

"Mind you she said there was drama one day.
I was shocked to the core!" she ventured to say
"I was bathing young Paul in the communal bath 'round tea

It was just getting dark; you won't believe me

From out of nowhere fish arrived with a splash
I don't know from where and how you might ask
I screamed and grabbed Paul and needless to say
Picked him up in a towel and ran home straight away

When John came from work, I said not a word
Although he could see something was wrong -that I was rather disturbed
He thought it was homesickness again so not a word was said
'Cause if John found the culprit, the bugger would be dead!

I never did tell John, but I can laugh at it now
Where the fish came from and exactly just how
They came in through that window which was really quite high."

"I have all your answers. At least let me try

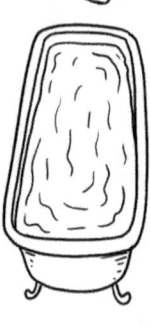

If I'd known it was you, the fish would have been straight in the bin
I can now well imagine the state you were in
It wasn't David Tiernan who I admit was quite big
Or his little brother Patrick who had the build of a twig

So I told her the story of fishing that day
With Patrick and David, good friends I must say
How the fish quickly rotted in the warm summer sun
And the antics of an eight-year-old who just wanted fun

Dedicated to Vera Bickerdike
A lifelong family friend. Born 31 March 1930 Died 24 July 2024

My Eyes Won't Open – 1959

It was time to have a little rest
To rest a weary head
A time for quiet and perhaps some sleep
Or so my teacher said

Lunch had been eaten
It was early afternoon
The camper beds were arranged
At the back of the classroom

The time dragged on forever
I was bored beyond belief
I closed my eyes and counted sheep
But couldn't find sleep

One day in absolute boredom
I played a 'harmless' little prank
With me eyelids shut I walked towards
The teacher named Miss Frank

"My eyes won't open!".
It was an innocent little lie
It seemed a good idea just then
Just to pass the time by

She picked me up and sat me down
Upon her wooden desk
My little legs were dangling over
the edge of where I sat

She gently touched each eyelid
She didn't want to poke or prod about
"It hurts me a lot," I told her.
I left her in no doubt

I heard her leave the room I think

MY EYES WON'T OPEN – 1959

The kids all sat so quietly
Was this the time to end the joke
I could end it now politely

She came back with the nun next door
She repeated the very same steps
They brought me cake and custard to eat
As if the food might help

With my eyes almost completely shut
I devoured the food quite quick
"I'm onto something worthwhile!" I thought
As a result of this harmless trick

Still, I kept both eyelids almost closed
Although I was getting a bit concerned
When would I end this little prank
It was getting a bit absurd

My older sister Catherine appeared
From 2 classes up the hall.
"She'll take you home. I think it's best"
Were the words I now recall

By now I was quite worried
I started to fret
Should I tell my sister Catherine
the truth?
I decided not yet

My sister held my little hand
As we walked to catch the bus
She was rather quiet and so was I
She wasn't one to fuss

The bus came by, and we got on board
Catherine led me down the aisle.
Some ladies apparently checked us out

MY EYES WON'T OPEN – 1959

And I quickly found out why

"Why are you crying little girl?"
"Because my little brother's blind!"
I wished the world would open up
And I could vanish deep inside

My mother was home and out the window she looked
She saw us walking up the street
Feeling the wall with my spare left hand
Walking slowly with my feet

We entered our house and my sister announced
The details of my plight.
My mother sceptical but not quite sure
About my disappearing sight

"Go to the toilet," It was upstairs
I climbed up rather slowly
On my hands and knees of course
With my mother watching surely

I looked in the mirror and forced a few tears
Confused about what to do
Should I confess to my sin of lying
(I was known to tell a few)

Back downstairs my mum picked me up
And on the kitchen bench I sat
A phone call was made I am pretty sure
I heard the purring of our cat

My heart skipped a beat when I clearly heard
The motor bike of my dad
My father was returning home to deal
With the nonsense of his lad

My eyes clenched shut my ears alert

MY EYES WON'T OPEN – 1959

I waited in fear of his arrival
He understood the workings of my mind
(In some ways he was a rival)

I didn't hear him silently step
Towards me now approaching
I strained to hear him, quite fearful now
My little heart exploding

He grabbed me with his big strong arms
And lifted me up to his face.
A short sentence he firmly shouted
Whilst held in this firm embrace

"If you don't open your eyes, it's to hospital you'll go,
And you'll stay a bloody fortnight!"
My tightly clenched eyes promptly opened wide
And in streamed the glorious daylight

He sat me down and walked off grinning
I expected to be in lots of trouble
But the world can be kind to a five-year old
Who lived in a bit of a bubble

Soon thereafter my mother read me the tale
Of the boy who once called Wolf
The warning was received both loud and clear
That it's best to stick with the truth.

2024

Dedicated to my loving sister Catherine.

Hot And Bothered

I was sticking to the vinyl couch
On a hot summer afternoon
The content on the TV bored me
A repeat of an old cartoon

My sister Julie sat fairly close to me
She was hot and bothered as well
She was also bored with the TV programme
I could very easily tell

Julie was in primary school
Quite shrewd and very bright
I decided to try a little prank on her
As older brothers might

I asked her to do me a favour,
And find my jumper without delay
"It'll help keep the hot air off me"
Was the explanation made

"That's silly. I don't believe you
More clothing will make you hotter."
She looked at me so convinced
And with the expression of a mocker

But she returned with my old brown jumper and
And I promptly put in on
It made me sweat a little more
Of that she wasn't wrong

"That's better and I thank you
I'm now feeling a lot less hot
Could you get me a scarf and a beanie?
It's working, I kid you not"

I added multiple layers of clothing

I was sweating underneath
I pretended to shiver uncontrollably
To confuse her firm belief

"I can see that you don't believe me
But I wouldn't lie to you!
I'm getting cooler by the minute.
And you should try this too!"

She looked at me fully sceptical
None of this made sense
It was surely all bluff on my part.
It is simply commonsense!

I said "If you don't believe me
There's a thermometer in the bathroom
 Find it and test my temperature
You should do this rather soon."

She went off quickly to the bathroom
I went promptly to the freezer
I took ice-cubes from a plastic tray
(I did it to deceive her)

No sooner was I back in the white chair
She was back with the scientific tool
If she could prove the lie I told her
She could call me out a fool

"You can stick it under my tongue," I said
You'll get a reading of my spit
Or you can put under armpits
It will very neatly fit

I pulled away some layers of clothes
And I did as she required
The thermometer went under my armpit
Where the ice-cubes did reside

I removed it in a minute
And gave her the scientific tool
It clearly told the truth of course
My arm pits were greatly less that cool

Julie stared at disbelief
At the temperature that it showed
It had dropped well below 10 degrees
But how, she didn't know

Julie shook her head in disbelief
She was annoyed and quite confused
How could the reading be so low?
I was feeling quite amused

I can't remember if I did confess
To this silly little prank
But it did distract the both of us
And for that we must give thanks.

2024

Dedicated to my loving sister Julie.

Year 9 Maths Lesson And The Hypnotist: 1970

Year 9 Maths was boring
We were anything but inspired
Mr. Ray was also bored
Though occasionally he tried

He had little passion in his teaching
At least that's how to us it seemed
The clock on the wall moved slowly
Through a window sunshine streamed

To avoid doing our morning lesson
We would try to distract him for a while

YEAR 9 MATHS LESSON AND THE HYPNOTIST: 1970

To get him completely off topic each lesson
We exercised some guile

One day it was my turn to distract him
And to delay the scheduled tasks
I knew he had some hobbies
So, I decided just to ask

"So apart from being in the Boy Scouts
Is there any else you like to do?"
(I pretended to be fully curious
As idiots will want to do)

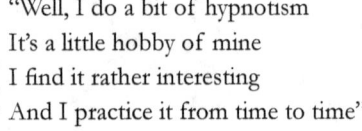

"Well, I do a bit of hypnotism
It's a little hobby of mine
I find it rather interesting
And I practice it from time to time"

The class was listening intently
To this harmless nice distraction
Could I stretch this out for a little while
And avoid the work on fractions?

"But hypnotism is just a con," I said.
"Just entertainment on TV
They just pretend to be hypnotized
From little that I see"

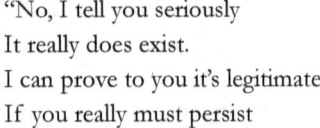

"No, I tell you seriously
It really does exist.
I can prove to you it's legitimate
If you really must persist

Do I have a volunteer
Who would like to be hypnotized?
I can do it here and now for sure
And right before your eyes"

YEAR 9 MATHS LESSON AND THE HYPNOTIST: 1970

Of course I put my hand up
This lesson was starting to be real fun
It would be a nice distraction
No harm could surely come!

He beckoned me to come forward
And I stood facing my captivated peers
He was just half a step behind me
And close to my left ear

"When I count to 10 I'll transform you
Into a solid plank of wood
(I should mention I was still very sceptical
In spite of where I stood)

The class was now fully captivated
He counted slow from 1 to 10
I stood erect in my foolish disbelief
And I winked to my classmate Ken

And when he finished counting
I stood with my arms cemented to my side.
To my surprise I couldn't move
No matter however hard I tried

Mr Ray picked up two chairs
And placed them as book ends
Somewhat apart with a gap in between
From whence I would suspend

Two boys helped him tilt me side-ways
And a chair was placed under my head
And then they placed my feet on the other chair
Just as Mr Ray said

"And now I'll prove the hypnotism
There's just one more thing to do
I want you all to come in single file

YEAR 9 MATHS LESSON AND THE HYPNOTIST: 1970

After you have taken off your shoes"

The obedient class lined up as he said
He gave them clear instructions
"Stand on his stomach and then step off.
From this chair and boy construction"

I was worried that I would just collapse
And fall between the chairs
Or that my back would break into little bits
In my mind I said a prayer

But, one by one my classmates
Quietly took their turn as told
Before stepping off on the other side
My body didn't buckle or even fold

In a minute or two it was all over
My terrifying ordeal
It confused me I must acknowledge
Was it a dream or was it real?

And then I was placed quite upright
I can honestly say it's true
I felt not a little twinge or any pain
As I honestly now tell you

He stood behind me once again
And counted back from 10
"You'll no longer be a plank of wood
You'll be normal once again"

There wasn't much time for Maths that lesson
My friends were happy for the distraction
In the playground no one doubted the veracity
Of how we dodged the work on fractions

At home I was keen to tell my nanna what happened

"I was hypnotized in class today"
"That's nice dear. Have a drink and a snack to eat
And just put your things away."

A Day At The Seaside – 1962

I could barely contain my excitement
I could barely sleep at night
A trip was planned to the seaside
A day of great delight

The hustle and bustle of the Station
People urgently to and fro
A trip to the sea on a steam train
Excitement overload!

We greeted cousins on the platform
The McCabes were meeting us there
A noisy reunion of children
Excitement in the air

The journey beings with steam train commotion
Billowing steam and mechanical noise
Parents smoking in cramped compartments
So many noisy girls and boys

We arrive at our destination
Saltburn by the Sea.
Or was it Redcar not so far away?
A hazy memory

Deckchairs hired and off with shoes
As we walked over stones complaining
The beckoning waves and cool offshore breeze
Rain for a while abstaining

The water took our breath away
As it lapped around our knees.

A DAY AT THE SEASIDE – 1962

Screams of delight and chattering teeth
The motion of cyclical seas

Flasks are opened and tea shared around
By the parents who watch and wave.
Trousers rolled up and arms exposed
As they pass the time of day

Us kids frolic in the water
The skin of some turns blue.
It's cold of course but accepted
(This may sound odd to you)

Eventually I become disconnected
I wander left and right
My short-sighted vision cannot discern
My parents are out of sight

The beach is packed, and I wander around
Trying to get my bearings
To find my tribe amongst the throng
Of humanity united

I wander into an enclosure
A man stands in careful attention
He's scanning the horizon for sharks or icebergs?
He seems right for my intention

In my nervous voice I ask for help
And I tell of my plight
He asks my name and age as well
He says that I'll be right

He makes a loud announcement
And mentions a boy named Stephen
Who is 5 years and rather lost
And could his parents now come and claim him?

A DAY AT THE SEASIDE – 1962

It's embarrassing to be lost to say the least
Was I just lacking in persistence?
But short-sighted Steve, you must believe
was in need of real assistance

Eventually my dad turned up.
He was only a short distance away
"It's Ok son." He smiles at me
And leads me on our way

Too soon it's time to just go home
But hunger and thirst prevail
The promise is made of fish and chips
On our way back to the train

We devour our chips like seagulls
Whilst sat up on some chairs
We grab and scoff the food like maniacs
Parents politely eating theirs

We scurry back to the station
It's now beginning to rain
We agree we've had a great time
And next year we'd come again

I sit in the comfort of my family
I'm feeling very tired
The rhythm of the train so soothing
As I gently close my eyes.

2025

Gosford Bank Visit – 1975

I loved to wear my body-shirt
I thought I looked so cool.
Skin-tight in a modern pale blue
I followed the fashion rule

The collars were a feature
And it didn't need a tie,
But occasionally I wore a wide one
To epitomize my style

And with my shorts and knee length socks
I'd strut in and out the court room
And up and down the main street
Celebrating youthful bloom

I had a variety of colours,
All rather hip and rather bold.
I thought I look a treat
If the truth be honestly told

One day I was asked to go to the local bank
To make the daily deposit
Of fines and payments, some cheques and cash
I said 'yes' and thought nothing of it

The bank was big and crowded
I was in a lengthy line
So I looked around and amused myself.
Whilst idly killing time

I spied a young man in the far distance
He was waiting too
He also was moving forward
To a teller not in my view

I had a good view of this young man

And I couldn't help but see
His physique was so wrong for a body shirt
He looked poor compared to me

Somone ought to tell him
He looked so weedy up from the waist
A body shirt looked so wrong on him
An absolute disgrace!

He reached the counter as I did
And then reality did strike
It was a mirror I'd been looking at
It was myself I'd didn't like!!

Despair and brutal recognition
A moment of painful realization
The body shirt was not for me
My rather sad frustration.

2025

Trains 1976 – Strathfield To Parramatta

It was just a normal morning
On a normal working day.
From Strathfield to Parramatta
In the usual travelling way

I walked to Strathfield Station
From my unit in Russell Street
I walked it every morning
In the cold and in the heat

I went to my normal platform
And sat where I'd normally sat
I only waited there just a minute or two
My train came along the track

And sure, enough it arrived on time
And quickly I was seated
And whilst travelling I read the paper
I travelled slightly overheated

But after the train reached Granville
It turned left instead of right
It turned southwards and not northwards
I felt a momentary fright

And so, I got off at the Maryland's platform
And went to the ticket man.
I explained the embarrassing situation
He was quick to devise a plan

"That's ok..just cross on the overhead bridge
And wait on that platform there
It will take you to back to Granville
Don't worry or despair"

So, I did that little manoeuvre
And was soon back at Granville Station
At platform 2 I hopped back on board
Without a look or hesitation

Once again, I arrived at Merrylands!
You can sense my extreme frustration
All I wanted was to get to work
And contribute to this nation

The ticket man was very surprised
To see me once again
He said the train at Platform 2 would usually go north
And he apologized for my pain

He added "it normally goes to Parramatta
But every now and again
It turns south to here at Merrylands ..

TRAINS 1976 – STRATHFIELD TO PARRAMATTA

I can't remember exactly when"

For the 2nd time I crossed the rail-line bridge
And was soon back at Granville station.
My anxiety had reached maximum
You can imagine my frustration

This time I checked the indicator board
This farce was almost beyond believing
It said Parramatta on Platform 4
A train was ready and just leaving

I sprinted down the stairs
And quickly hopped on board
Just as the door were closing
With my calmness partly restored

But no! the disaster continued
I was back at Merrylands station!!
Perhaps the board had been changed a minute too soon
And now more humiliation!!

I couldn't face the ticket man
I just couldn't take the chance
My newspaper covered my face
And I left without a glance

I was done with trains that morning
Beyond the point of exasperation
The joke had gone on far too long
I'd had enough of Merrylands Station!!

I walked out of the Merrylands Station
And crossed the busy street
I hopped inside the closest cab
And admitted my defeat

"Where to?" the driver asked me.

"To the court-house at Parramatta."
We filled in the several minute journey
Without the usual morning chatter

Then he said, "I've taken you there before I think."
He said in mistaken recognition
I assured him that wasn't the case and
this was a one-way expedition

So if God or life conspires one day
To make an absolute fool of you
You'll eventually see the funny side
If you take the wiser point of view…

2025

Bin Night

Richard Glover writes an article or two
And he made laugh today
He wrote of the bin obsession of older men
As they gradually fade away

The article made me chuckle
Because I don't obsess about bins
Yes, I have other quirks of nature
And possibly other sins

Ray used to be the street general
He never failed to know
What bins went out on Thursday night
General waste, recycling and FoGo

He'd put his bins out early
It was a signal for us all
The whole street trusted him completely
Of this I do recall

BIN NIGHT

But Ray died a few years ago
And has gone to that recycling plant in the sky
I decided it was time to take his place
Or at least give it a decent try

I was keen to be the street general
And I started right away
I put my two bins out early
On a rainy winter's day

The residents of my street soon followed me
Their bins soon were placed kerbside
As I thought of my good friend Raymond
I had a tear within my eye

And just about time to go to bed
My dear wife saw the errors of my folly
I had both the bins completely wrong
So out I went with my brolly

On her advice I rectified
The mistakes I had clearly made
I did the job that I should have done
A few hours earlier, that day

And in the morning my bins were emptied
But the street was in disarray
It was an embarrassing spectacle of ineptitude
With only myself to blame

I secretly thought it was hilarious
Though it wasn't an intended prank
I now rely on my wife's good judgement
And for that, I give her thanks.

2025

Trains: The Minister Speaks

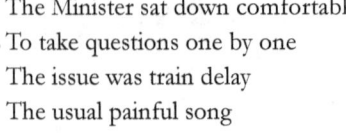

The Minister sat down comfortably
To take questions one by one
The issue was train delay
The usual painful song

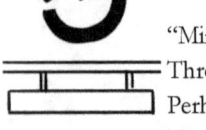

"Minister, 1 in 5 trains have problems
Throughout our entire state
Perhaps we need a task force
To thoroughly investigate?

And there are issues with industrial action
They continue unabated
We seemed close to resolution
Or was it simply overstated?"

"I hear exactly what you're saying
And I don't wish to minimize
The disruption to the services
That is frequent on our lines

But the late train issue has a silver lining
If you'll bear with me a while
It's not doom and gloom for every-one,
I'll explain the reason why

Say you missed your train at 10am
You're annoyed, I understand
Your frustration level may then rise
I can see just where you stand

But the person who arrives just later
Sees the train that is running late
But for him that train is early
God's will or simply fate?

He or she arrives early

TRAINS: THE MINISTER SPEAKS

With a smile upon their face
The other passenger arriving late perhaps
At their designated place

To simply say that trains are late
Is an unwise simplification.
Perhaps it's a question of attitude
Without need of rectification?

It evens out quite nicely
Over an extended period of time.
You can win and lose on journeys
As if intended by design

We are living in the modern age.
This is where we're at
It pays to be quite flexible
as we pivot and adapt"

The journalist went silent
She took a call on another line.
The minister sat serenely
Just quietly passing time

"Minister, we have an angry caller
Who would like to speak to you
Due to a train delay she missed surgery
Not just on one hip, but on two"

"I'd love to take that call
I can image her frustration
But I really must leave for an interview
At another TV station"

So, I really must get going.
I so wish I could take that call.
Please pass on my sincere hope
she doesn't have another fall

Ask her to call my office
My staff will do everything they can
Tomorrow I'm heading overseas
To see trains in north Japan"

So why not arrive at your train station
At a totally random time
And catch a train to anywhere,
For a journey so sublime?

2015

Plumber Wants A Partner

It's prime time viewing for millions
On commercial television
Tom The Plumber on a quest for love
For a marriage made in heaven

Seven would-be brides converged
And arrived at a chosen location
It was at a plumber's shed in Sutherland
Just up from the local station

Some nervous introductions
And meals at the Boyles Hotel
Each girl tried to win his heart
Especially Isabelle

It made for tense television
As viewers clearly took sides
Girls one by one were painfully rejected
There were tears in many eyes

Tom struggled to make a final choice
It was either Tracey or Stephanie
Tracey had an engaging smile
And was mid-way in her degree

And Stephanie was in dentistry
Tom was clearly interested.
He'd been having grief with a molar tooth
With surgery more than once suggested

The viewing ratings climbed each week
So much workplace speculation!
Would Tom The Plumber find true love?
It was the talk of half the nation!

And as for Tom's final choice
you should just tune in every week.
There's such great television
about the love that plumbers seek

And if you love a good tense drama
In the lounge room of your house.
There's also "Farmer Wants a Wife" or
"Sparky Seeks a Spouse!"

June 2025

Worms For Dinner

My mum was becoming annoyed
As I prodded with my fork
It was taking me ages to eat my lunch
The mincemeat was beef or pork

I steered the mince around my plate
From one side to the other
I was passive but non-compliant
I sensed frustration in my mother

"You need to eat your dinner.
Your dinner is going cold
The mince is nice and healthy
Just please do as you're told"

WORMS FOR DINNER

"What's this next to the meaty bits?"
They look like little garden worms
I'll eat the meat but leave those bits
I think I saw one just now squirm!"

"You're looking at cooked onion bits
I wouldn't put worms inside the mince!
Onions add flavour to the mincemeat!"
I sat there unconvinced.

"If I eat all the mashed potato
And all the mincemeat that I like
Can I leave behind the onions
And go outside and ride my bike?"

She sighed and nodded in agreement
We reached a compromise of sorts
So, I poked around with the tip of my knife
I stayed there deep in thought

My mum was looking even more annoyed
She stood to leave the dining room
She walked into the kitchen
To wash the dishes, I presumed

I loved my mashed potato
I'd happily eat it every day,
But today I had to make a sacrifice
If I was going to get my way

I used my knife to excavate
From inside the pile of mash
A cave was fashioned with lots of room
The mince went in in just a flash

I made a little potato door
To hold the mince inside
The remaining mash was wonderful

Problem solved and with some pride

I carried my plate into the kitchen
And showed just a pile of mash
"The mince was nice just as you said,"
As I walked towards the trash

I'll just scrape the mash into the bin
And give you my dirty plate
Thanks for lunch it was really nice.
I'm sorry for being so late"

And after just a little while,
Say an hour at the very most
I'd have jam and bread on nice white bread
Perhaps even on some toast!

August 2025

Dedicated to my loving mum, Mary Leonard.

The Leg Cramp

I was putting on my trackies
But I didn't point down my toes
My foot got wedged just halfway down
With nowhere else to go

I decided to push down harder
And force my right foot through
It was a futile attempt if the truth be known
I must confide in you

The pushing and efforts were useless
They were an exercise in futility
Upon reflection I should just have sat down
And avoided my stupidity

Instead In a moment of pure 'genius'
I decided to raise my foot behind me
So I could grab handful of the tracksuit leg
And remove it quick and simply

That's when the leg cramp stuck so deadly
And now I was almost crying
I clenched my teeth as I quietly swore
Could this be worse than dying?

I hopped across the bathroom
It was not a pretty sight
I stumbled to the bathroom stool
Where I continued with this fight

I managed to remove the rest of the trackies
So now I was sitting barely dressed
Then I was able to stretch the leg
Such relief I must confess

These little tribulations
If the truth be honestly told
Are episodes of the advancing years
And the joy of growing old!

Henry The Dog

If I were 4 decades younger
Without love or a true soul mate
I'd borrow the pup called Henry
I would be dumb to hesitate

Henry is a labrador
He's only 6 months old
He belongs to my sister Julia
To her the pup was sold

HENRY THE DOG

I'd train him with little treats
'Cause he likes a snack or two
He's smart and irresistible
I should confide in you

And on the walking tracks
We'd begin our little quest
We'd keep our eyes wide open
As we surveyed the very best

Once we have picked the special lady
We begin to execute the plan
We make a beeline towards our quarry
This team of dog and desperate man

I'd pretend to nobly restrain him
As if trying to hold him back
He'd wag his tail quite furiously
As we stopped upon the track

I'd apologise profusely
"He won't cause you any harm
He must find you so attractive
And with a special type of charm"

And during this conversation
Henry would use his puppy eyes
He'd press right up against her leg
In his quest to captivise

And by way of offering apology
I'd offer her a coffee or some tea.
If she had a spare half hour
To spend with Henry and also me

Is this lacking in dating ethics?
I suspect it just might be
I managed without the likes of Henry

In my vivid memory

I got the girl I wanted
I admit it took a while
She has her share of natural beauty
With abundant Italian style

But if you can't find your soul mate
You might consider a special type of dog
Who will help you in your quest for love
On your daily walk or jog.

2025

PART B

The Aussie Jesus

This Jesus was an Aussie
He drove a Holden ute
He had a dog named Bruiser
Old and not too cute

He worked around the outback
and spun a yarn or two
He gave advice and handy hints
'bout what a bloke should do

He'd chew the fat, had time for kids
Was nice to those in need.
Not so nice to the 'two-faced'
And to those consumed with greed

He told the tale of a jackaroo
Who was robbed and left for dead.
The local vicar passed him by
so, the story said

He didn't stop or offer help
and left in an almighty state
Saying something about meeting someone
Or something that couldn't wait

An hour later a Gunggari man came
and seeing the jackaroo
he stopped to lend a helping hand
as good neighbours want to do

He brought the injured jackaroo
to the hospice that very night
and left a few quid to pay the bills
to 'see the doctor right'

Jesus liked a beer 'most every day.

THE AUSSIE JESUS

Some said he drank too much
whilst sipping on their chardonnay
quite chilled and with their lunch

He learnt a thing or two from native men
about native remedies,
about treating scabs and aching joints
in arms or dodgy knees

He had no time for hypocrites
Or those who preached with style
These folks he said "up themselves
at least a country mile"

He came into town one night they say.
They said it was a trap.
He'd rubbed some folks up pretty bad,
this normally peaceful chap

The did him in behind the pub
behind the "Light Horse Cavalry."
They left him dead or beaten up
but in truth I did not see

He's not seen much around the town these days.
Some say he's actually gone
but others say he's still around
The rumours are quite strong

Most good folk do shed a tear
and fondly do recall
The things that Jesus said and did
His words for one and all

And Bruiser, well he's now a stray
Of sorts but with many friends
Every decent folk and family
Do lend a helping hand

He's often at the nursing home
Or the hospice for the kids
His popularity has just grown and grown
But are the followers quite his?

All the men who drink in town
Who spit and say "who gives…"
Have written upon their utes or arms
The words that "Jesus Lives!"

2012

The Clash Of Two Kingdoms – Palm Sunday

Matthew 21:1-11

When Alexander came to Jerusalem
about 300 years BC
he really made an entrance
and they gathered there to see

With the sun shining so brightly,
on his armour polished well
on a white stallion so impressive.
So majestic above the swell

With a plume upon his helmet
a warrior king for sure,
In the days before stretch limos
such a sight for the rich and poor

He proclaimed his earthly power
and in his appearance, one could see
his proud and noble features,
Whilst he thought "all just look at me!"

THE CLASH OF TWO KINGDOMS - PALM SUNDAY

The conquered paid him homage
without a thought of what it cost
It was an alliance of the mighty
And its meaning was not lost

And when Pompey entered the city
About 6 decades before JC,
the Roman left not the slightest doubt
about his claim for majesty

But when Jesus entered Jerusalem
not a limo could be seen!
no wealth or power symbols
no pride or earthy gleam

He picked the humblest choice of transport,
not a horse but a donkey
and a colt there right beside her
to keep her company

He straddled them both quite carefully,
and kept them side by side
The crowd thought it hilarious,
"Hosanna!" they all cried

It was like an old VW beetle,
with Jesus in the driving seat.
with a towrope pulling it forward
in the midday scorching heat

And Jesus waved excitedly,
whilst taking quite the piss
of vain and wordly leaders
who are often quite remiss

His enemies were quite furious,
within in their lofty towers,
as they looked upon this farcical

mocking of earthly powers

How dare he be so defiant!
How dare he mock our type!
How dare he give no value!
To our power, wealth and hype

The crowd enjoyed his theatre
They loved his entrance style
They called to him "Hosanna!"
They yelled for quite a while

He knew that crowds are fickle
And from this moment of comic relief
A crowd can change in the blink of any eye,
And become a source of grief

And when he finally passed them
after entering through the gate,
he gathered with his apostles
There was little time to wait

And gathering with those closest
He said, "well, now I'm here."
And if you stared at him intently
There was the surest glimpse of fear.

2014

My Last Christmas

I'm looking through my bedroom window,
I see them sitting there
around the outdoor table,
relaxed and in their chairs

The casual conversation
the easy gentle chat

MY LAST CHRISTMAS

The joy of their reunion
I know just where they're at

I'm attempting to stay detached
from my 60 years of wife
I try to avoid the tenseness
the anger and the strife

Ours was never an easy marriage
but we sort of muddled through
some peace and some confrontation
As most couples seem to do

But lately it's impossible
Because of frustration and bitterness
The last days of our long lifetimes
and perhaps our last Christmas

It's a curse to be so frail
and so advanced in earthly years
My mind and body struggling
with the burden of my fears

This house is now a prison
We can barely leave our home
No friendly visitations
We're feeling quite alone

The 2 weeks in respite care
I honestly have to say,
were so pleasant and so easy
Each and every day

A daughter tries her hardest
but she can barely cope
Another daughter has just separated
and with it all her hope

So, to you my friendly neighbours
May you enjoy this festive season
'Cause there's little joy for me right now
I'm bereft of hope and reason.

2018

I've Become Invisible

I've become invisible
to the mighty powers that be
with their backs now turned towards me
whilst sipping on their tea

Once I was very visible
in my shirt and matching tie
with that careless chat and handshakes
and that knowing practiced smile

I took a step quite risky
based on strong beliefs
I challenged those more senior
So, I copped my share of grief

I lost a battle but won the war
It took some time to see
that being a 'hotshot' in a smart suit
was not my destiny

2016

Luke 18:16-17

It was a day they'll all remember.
One fabulous peaceful day
when adults of all ages
decided they would play

Dentists and accountants
housewives, gardeners too,
downed their tools of trade that day
to see what they could do

Parliament went outside that day
and played handball in the street.
Bob Hawk was rather agile
and light upon his feet

A Bishop roared with laughter
upon some swings in the city park.
Sinners, bankers, brokers
they stayed there until dark

Yes, sure there were some upsets
One judge didn't get his way
so he sulked off to a corner
and stayed there half the day

The children were quite marvellous
the grown-ups did agree
they taught them rules and how to play
and gave them morning tea

They served them lunch at 1 o'clock
Nutella on white bread!
Though accustomed to much finer food
not one complaint was said

LUKE 18:16-17

Soldiers used their rifles
as useful cricket bats
Some children drove their tanks through town
they joked and laughed at that

Lawyers, post-men, housewives
rode bikes up streets and lanes
They walked them up the steeper hills
Their muscles felt the strain

The shadows slowly lengthened
but still the grown-ups played
They'd never known such fun they said
Though hungry each one stayed

The streetlights came on finally
The children called them in
Bathed, fed and tucked in bed
A smile up each chin

The children met and said the day
had been a great success
no one murdered, raped or shot
no fraud or brokenness

It was a day they'll all remember
with warmth for quite a while
when grown-ups remembered childhood
and God was seen to smile.

2014

My Dad And The Cockroach

We forged a new life in Australia
We came midyear '63
We'd left dear old England
my family and me

The desolation is distant now
My father died when I was 11
I heard my little sister cry
and "daddy's gone to heaven"

I wrote that verse in a dream one night
One a balmy summer night
I awoke to kill a cockroach
in my bed with quite a fright

I punched the little critter
to the relief of my dear wife
The cockroach was no quitter
but I ended its brief life

Life can be very brutal
Death so swift it leaves you stunned
As if caught in some mad battle
where you find yourself outgunned

But forged amongst the heartache
you toughen up like steel
You find some strength and resilience
whilst gasping on your knees

So, thank you Mr Cockroach!
Some ideas were in my head
whilst I did slumber that warm summer night
and you died upon my bed

MY DAD AND THE COCKROACH

The battlefields are many
in our heart and in our minds
My dad and the Cockroach,
their fate on earth unkind

My dad resides with Jesus now
Of that I have no doubt
The cockroach, I'm not sure about
I'll let God work that one out

It's now just on 4am
I really need to sleep
But this poem was in my dreams tonight
I know I must complete

My wife may be asleep now.
She hates these creepy-crawlies,
who invaded out beds and our dreams tonight
Our peaceful dreamtime stories

So, thank you to the Cockroach
You made this verse quite possible
Yes, you died by my own one fist tonight
The force was just unstoppable!

And thank you dad for this gift of verse
My funny Irish dad!
You were the best I could have hoped for
The very best I could have had.

2018

I Have This Sinking Feeling

I have this sinking feeling
in my glossy 5th floor flat.
It's a depressing situation
But that's just where I'm at

The cracks are in the basement
And up an outside wall
I left my home a week ago
It was such a painful call

I have this sinking feeling
and the engineers said it's true
We're slowly sinking downwards
I'm feeling oh so blue

I have a rash, I cannot sleep
I don't know what to do
Financial ruin is quite likely
With no prospect should we sue

It's a powerless situation
and I don't know who to blame
developers or the builders?
I think they're all the same

The new apartment across the road
has blocked my water view
but their owners now look worried
Perhaps they're sinking too?

My 5th floor is sinking downwards
It seems so sad to me
I'll be no longer share the 5th floor
More likely number 3

2019

Blackbird

There's a blackbird in my garden
and he's got a sniff of sun
He is singing his little heart out
as the day has just begun

As I have morning cuppa
I consider the morning news
but it's mostly only discord
and I catch the morning blues

So, I write him this little verse
Little does he know
whilst on a branch outside my window
as the winter breeze does blow

There's a Butcherbird in the distance
A call cute with a semitone hook
I wish he'd come a bit closer
So, I could take a better look

I wish I knew their language
And what it might all mean
Do they call and hope for romance?
You know just what I mean

Every morning holds some promise
Of what a day might give
Some joy in the daily cycle
Good reason just to live.

2019

My Nose – Part 2

I looked into the mirror
And saw upon my nose
A growth upon the left nostril
The colour of a rose

It's just a pimple I said in comfort
No need to really worry
It will be gone in just a day or two
No need for haste or scurry

Two days later I re-inspected
A yellow pussy sight I saw
A remedy was close to me
With a toothpick in my claw

I jabbed it in the middle
And the pressure was released
It squirted out quite freely
I was more than just relieved

I squeezed it hard till blood appeared
A sign that all was good
As I irrigated the pimple
As all irrigators should

Then a little bit of Tea Tree oil
To kill those nasty germs
That conspire to ruin my youthful looks
For which I sometimes yearn

I thought this was the end of grief
And went about my way
But the redness did return again
But why? I could not say

I repeated the procedure
With a little more intent
Could this be a nuisance skin-cancer?
For a skin check I then went.

2020

Nursing Home Blues

I'm in a bloody nursing home
It's driving me insane
The loneliness, the sense of decay.
Each day is just the same

I cry myself to sleep each night
And I sleep for some respite
But the dreams, they really haunt me
They can last for most the night

The food tray is on a trolley
It's been there half a day
But without any mobility
It could be a million miles away

The picture in the photograph
Shows a man with wit and pride
The mirror now reveals an image
So sad I can but cry

We're all in this together
The aged and the insane
With dementia swarming all around us
A wave of fear and pain

The news showed a young fatality
A man, a bike and a tree
He lost control and is now quite dead.
I'm filled with real envy

The staff have muted spirits
The writing is on the wall
They know what's coming to them
In a decade or two, that's all

I used to have such standards
Of dress and self-hygiene.
But the whiff of what's in my pull-ups
just makes me want to scream

We're surrounded by televisions
and our chairs are faced that way
We stare at a screen for hours on end
Just another wasted day.

2020

Tribute To The Whistleblowers

The whistleblower stands defiant
beaten but not quite broken
The consequences of a battle
Over words of truth once spoken

It started with pricks of conscience
Of things not appearing right
A perception of lost direction
Those sleepless restless nights

A meeting of disquiet
With tension in the air
Analysis on the table
Trying to seem so fair

The truth is very obvious
Why do they refuse to see
The problems are enormous
And why visible just to me?

TRIBUTE TO THE WHISTLEBLOWERS

The senses of isolation
Overwhelming day and night
The questions of one's judgment
To awake with such a fright

Now subject to micro-supervision
With 'faults' found her and there
HR 'concerns' about 'performance'
The frequent hostile stare

It's easy to wreck a reputation
It's hardly rocket science
An unfair workload with 'white-anting'
Then concerns about compliance

No longer in the 'in-crowd"
No friendly chats with drinks
These questions of 'performance"
The spirit slowly sinks

A rather quick work-place exit
It feels like sharp disgrace
Some moments of real self-doubt
It's written on the face

This emptying of the work-place
The desk and cupboards bare
The removal of family photos
And yes, it is unfair

It's a Good Friday crucifixion
A real Jesus imitation.
The sacrifice of a humble lamb
And shame upon our nation

The sacrifice now completed
With the body on the cross
Not even eventual vindication

Can remove this sense of loss

And after becoming so invisible
There is no final glory
No apology or reconciliation
Little daylight in this story

2020

The Marathon

They nursed me so tenderly
I was their pride and joy
We started the race so long ago
I was their only boy

The spectators on the sideline
They watched me slowly grow
They watched my daily milestones
It was so long ago

After a while my feet were grounded
I ran with my family
I ran with reckless abandon
My family and me

The spectators cheered and urged us on
My steps grew big and stronger
My parents were now behind me
My strides were now much longer

Familiar faces on the sideline
Some older family members
Now deceased but still involved
Their faces, I remember

I saw my father falter
I was only just eleven

THE MARATHON

But still he cheered and urged me on
From the sideline that was heaven

At time the mist enclosed me
I hardly knew the way
Sometimes it's hard to make some sense of
The meaning of tough days

The hills were very challenging
I truly gasped for air
My family mostly with me
I sensed their love and care

At times I was unsure of
The course that was ahead of me
Some confusion and uncertainty
Of the path of my destiny

And then there were the downhill runs
With speed I picked up pace
The faces either side of me
I recognised each face

The spectators grew in number
Some family members smiling
They started the race once with me
But now were on the sidelines

At times I truly stumbled
I fell but did recover
I picked myself up from the ground
Of myself I did discover

I stopped and turned and faced behind me
As I took my final steps
Some brokenness and disappointment
Some failures not addressed

THE MARATHON

I knew I could have done more
I could have given and not taken
My generosity at times lacking
A chance or two forsaken

But mostly satisfaction
I've passed the character test
Some humility and contrition
The sense of being quite blessed

I see I am a solo runner
My parents present but not running
My kids and wife behind me
I see them, they are coming

It's my time to cross the finish line
I gave it all I've got
The marathon almost finished
I think my legs are shot

There's a cheer of jubilation
The joy is worth the pain
It was a journey well worth travelling
I'd do it all again

Having crossed the finish line
My weariness deserts me
The embrace of those who cheered me on
their love I feel sublimely.

My Feet

They operate in confined spaces
Where its sweaty, cramped and hot
They never whinge, grip and curse, I think
And complain about their lot

I now thank my toes individually
I really should know them all by name
And though I am in that sense remiss
I thank them all the same

Today they get the attention
That is very much overdue
I soak them in a small tub
It's the least that I can do

After minutes in a hot tub
With water warm and soapy
They are looking grand and rather pristine
No longer sad and dopey

A little bit of TLC
It's a wonderful investment
I sense their appreciation
No hint of their resentment

For all the punishment I gave them
For those toes I should have loved
For the blisters I've inflicted
I say sorry to God above

They've never expressed any jealousy
About the care I take with hands
They've got on with their daily tasks
They accept and understand

They've taken me to Everest
That journey took a while
And after I met my Ernie
They walked me down the aisle

Let's hear it for the quiet achievers
Those who make our lives complete
No fanfare, self-praise or boasting
A tribute, to our feet.

2020

Funeral for a Friend

A life cut short in the prime of her life
A mother, a daughter, a colleague, a wife

A gathering of many, a rousing goodbye
The tributes, the prayers and still we ask why?

A life extinguished in a moment of time
The briefest of illness. Bad luck not a crime

A tear for her daughters in my eyes I could tell
Her husband, her loved ones, her neighbours as well

But for the grace of God I go, I hear some folk say
As if God plays a game on who is to stay

On those who die early and those who do not
As if God is selective…I think it's all rot

Because fate spins most surely on the roll of a dice
We skate unbeknown on the thinnest of ice

We all do it daily we acknowledge the chance
And when we see danger, we still choose to dance

To live life with all caution just keeping quite safe

FUNERAL FOR A FRIEND

Is a life not worth living. We have to be brave

Christ told his followers to pick up their cross
To follow him bravely, but yes, there's a cost

And a tear for the young boy just 11 years old
My young former self and a story untold

The same sudden illness, for him bleed in the brain
The death of my father so hard to explain

The numbness at the funeral shell-shocked to the core
A coffin, a service I can barely recall

The same winter's morning cold and so bleak
With my mother and sisters for those I now speak

The pain and desolation that's hard to explain
Or spoken of easily without re-living the pain

Memories resurface in some funerals I attend
Not those of the elderly in those I contend

Advanced in years it's sad I agree
But not quite that tragedy today that I see

Your hearts were quite broken as you stood by the car
The grief and the anguish. I could sense it afar

But love will one day triumph. I know this is true
And hearts slowly lighten, and I say this now to you

Her laughter, great memories, they float around like a feather.
New life shines through darkness when you think that it might never

Your mother has given you three, the finest of treasure
Her everlasting love will last you all forever.

2020

The Angel

The angel went from bed to bed
"She spoke so warmly to each," they said

"She held some hands and eased some fears,
And wiped away the occasional tears"

She didn't know them but could sense their fear
She took a chair and sat quite near

She spoke quite softly to some they said
As she did the rounds from bed to bed

"There's no need to fear or have fear of dying
Let's face it…life is trying

I've seen it twice with 2 good men
I've seen the end and said Amen"

My mum's operation was just a day away,
And I wondered if it was just a delay

The details were lacking over the phone
When I took the call before leaving my home

My mother's fate had been finally sealed
A growth in her lungs the test revealed

She wanted home and her family near
She made her decision abundantly clear

Being a weekend, the doctors weren't there,
But my mother, to be honest, just didn't care

A staff member resisted. My mum said, "whatever for?
Just watch me walk soon out that door."

We chatted as we left in my car
The journey home was a little bit far

She gave me an update. She told me the facts
She seemed quite at peace and completely relaxed

"I decided today to just leave the place
There was quite a reaction from face to face

I wasn't trying to upset the staff
In fact, one or two enjoyed a laugh"

"Those poor girls in there were so full of dread,
So I did the rounds from bed to bed

We had a laugh and an honest chat
We spoke of life and this and that"

I remembered the words of the nurse at the desk
"Your mum is an angel ..one of the best

You take good care of her from here,
In the months ahead as death draws near."

It's nearly twenty years since we said goodbye.
Those memories so clear of that day in my mind.

2023

Dedicated to my loving mum Mary Leonard, 1930 to 1995.

Jock Martin

7:30 Report 24th March. 2021

Jock Martin is a hero
He hails from Manning Point
And when the local feared flooding
He vowed to get them out

He runs the local bowling club
He is loved by one and all

JOCK MARTIN

He is a leader in a community
He responded to their call

He used a tractor with a bucket
He carried them without fail
He carried them to safety
they all lived to tell the tale

He organised a helicopter
To bring in medical supplies
The locals owe him everything
There are tears in their soft eyes

Jock doesn't wear a well-cut suit
He doesn't drive in a government car
He seldom seeks the media
Not known by those afar

On that island in the Manning River
Not remote in a Canberra bubble
Jock goes about his daily life
Not a sniff of Canberra trouble

So go Jack, down to Canberra
And you show them how it's done
Show the authentic leadership
Your time has surely come

Teach them about integrity
And manhood and dignity
About honest conversation
And not the nonsense that we see

Run workshops in the lunchtime
Make them strictly compulsory
For the Swinging Dicks of Canberra
(But they sound more like pricks to me)

Teach them leadership in the real sense
About service of community
Not the booze and sex subculture
That we see on our TV

And teach them about humility
You teach them well and good
And tell them we are disgusted
Hang their heads they should.

2021

The Early Morning Walk – The Blue Mile

It's the perfect way to start the day
To begin your day with style
You should start the day with a morning walk
You should walk at least a mile

But to maximise your experience
A few hints and some advice
You might think that I'm pedantic
Or perhaps not so very nice

So first you need your earbuds
Bluetooth is best, I know
Then click on your favourite playlist
And now it's almost time to go

But seaweed can get smelly
It can be such an offensive smell
And there's the stuff that dogs deposit on paths
We all know this very well

So, some filters up each nostril
I think is good advice
Admit the fact the some of the smells
Are hardly very nice

Then you'll need a pair of dark sunnies
You can wear them night or day
You should wear them to avoid eye-contact
With those you pass along the way

And since Covid is still lurking
A mask to cover your mouth
Those Covid germs are back in Sydney
And I hear they're heading south

So, get out there now and enjoy yourself
And get fit along the way!
Such a wonderful sensory experience
The perfect start each day.

2024

The Player

He made your life a misery,
From the time you both did wed
He left you cold at nighttime,
When he slept in other beds

The womanizing, his errant ways
They said he was 'a lad'
The grins and winks from his drinking mates
The 'good times' that he had

You kicked him out. He pleaded
He promised to repent
He yearned to be a family man.
His wild oats were surely spent?

And then you welcomed babies
For a while he seemed at peace
There was a glimmer of possibility
That his reckless ways would cease

THE PLAYER

And then the reckless ways resumed
His promises and proclamation
That he didn't love the others,
'It was just sex..no complication"

The despair surely took hold
Of your mind and of your heart
With the promise of a new life
From England you did depart

The sun might is stronger in Australia
But problems still remained.
His bad behaviour continued
No sign of his restraint

Your anxiousness and worry
Thoughts of impending doom
His temper short and on a fuse
The atmosphere of gloom

The tablets from the doctors
It's true, did ease your pain
They numbed the desolation.
The issues still remained

The marriage rolled on through the years.
Your heart an empty shell
He made your life a misery,
Your friends could easily tell

Locked cupboards in the kitchen
Your money stashed away
His cruelty perplexed you
You wondered why you stayed

You supported him in his decline,
As expected of a wife
It was not love as motivation,

THE PLAYER

But your sense of duty in this life

And when you fell into that abyss
Your mental health quite gone,
Dementia or a break down?
There was something very wrong

He visited you in hospital
You attacked him with all your might.
Decades of anger and resentment
You were spoiling for a fight

He decided to play the victim card
"How can she act this way?
After everything I've done for her!"
The doctors said.. 'don't stay'

He broke your spirit and your heart
You are almost an empty shell
You exist as a tragic victim
Of a lifetime living hell

He is an utter waste of space
That's all that I need to say
For him, forget redemption
Just inevitable decay.

2020

Musical Chairs

Trump, Putin and Zelensky

Three men circled the table
There were only chairs for two
When the music stopped, a scramble took place
With an unholy alliance of two

No one wanted to be left standing
Alone and solitary exposed
Alone without an alliance
The dancers were light on their toes

Whist the music played it was frantic
Yelling and insults flew fast
Promises made and retracted
How long will this chaos last?

Innocent observers were left speechless
As alliances were hastily abandoned
The frantic desperate lunges
With one dancer doomed to be stranded

The audience is simply dumbfounded
And ask "what the hell now is going on?
The promises made quite recently
Are now almost certainly gone!

What to make of this weird calamity
So bizarre and crazy to see
Who are the goodies and baddies
what will the future be?

A changing landscape of allies
One minute foe and then the best friend
What of the old alliances
Just how will this mad dance end?

Truth is reversed in a second
Lies told without the blink of an eye
The order of things is upended
We wonder and can't help but ask why?

Orwell will take note in his gravesite
He predicted and feared this would be
The turmoil, the angst and confusion
Uncertainty now guaranteed.

2025

The Disrupter

He ignored and dismissed the notion
That young aspiring Rabbi's should be recruited
to preach about his Heavenly father
He thought them generally unsuited

So, he recruited around the Sea of Galilee
that shimmering inland sea
where working class men just plied their trade
And fished for their community

He recruited, it seems, fairly easily
He gave tips on how to fish
Though he himself was hardly a fisherman
they followed as he wished

The fishermen were receptive to new thinking
On what mattered and what was real
He spoke the language of his people
Essential truths revealed

About God, his heavenly father
Who loves the humble and the meek
a disruption of conventional thinking
challenging the power elite

THE DISRUPTER

His parables had weird endings
That made his audience really ponder.
A father forgives his prodigal son?
A Samaritan despised no longer?

He entered Jerusalem in crazy fashion
Mathew said he rode upon donkey and her offspring
And whilst he sat riding upon both creatures
"Hosanna!" the crowd did sing

And then to rub salt into some open wounds
He upturned tables for all to see
The corrupt temple of Jerusalem
An ungodly travesty

He took some bread and wine one day
And said to those gathered close around him
This is my body and blood take head
For some that was quite astounding

He preferred prostitutes and tax collectors
over the company of the strong and proud.
Social status meant not a thing to him
Earthly honours now disavowed

He healed the sick on the Sabbath
and Pharisees questioned "why?"
He rebuked their clever arguments
So, they decided he should die

And that's the nature of disrupters.
They offer you the ride that's wild and fast
White knuckled as you just hang on
And how long will this journey last?

They throw out the usual rule book
The past no longer rules the present
It's either a journey up to the highest peak

Or deep down in a scary descent

A messiah or an antichrist?
It's kinda hard to tell.
Will we be delivered to Utopia
Or to a derivative of hell?

History and God alone will judge them
When we are either liberated or in prison
Whether the disruptor left us either tied in chains
Or enthralled with a heavenly vision

And over the centuries, at least a millennium,
we compartmentalize, sanitize and make benign
the wild teaching of the disrupter
It's often happens over time.

2025

The Morning Announcement

The department head Mr Roger Bentley
announced at morning tea,
"I thank Gillian from our HR team
For this groundbreaking policy

In response to empirical data
And after paying for a consulting team
Certain changes warrant implementation
Of this policy I now reveal

Apparently, the department has been remiss
To notice an unfair trend
Short staff had been overlooked
This injustice will shortly end

A 40/40/20 policy will be implemented immediately
And it will be enforced from today quite strongly

THE MORNING ANNOUNCEMENT

We will remedy those promotions
That in the past were made so wrongly

The staff nodded in agreement
Especially by those quite short
The taller looked a bit sheepish
Having benefitted from a previous rort

"Head office has advised quite clearly
That 40% and not less
Will be filled by those vertically challenged
To remedy this dreadful mess

And for those 182cm and taller
An allocation fair and just
Their number will be exactly 40%
Your support for this, I trust"

A hand went up, and a man stood to speak
"That leaves another 20
Who will constitute this number
I ask you Mr Bentley?"

"I'm so glad you asked this question
And I thank you Henry Calder
It will be filled in part by shorter people
Who identify as being taller

And to show we haven't forgotten
Those who are like our very own Ms Bittle
By that I mean those rather tall
Who identify as being little

Our policies will be a beacon
For the country as a whole
Please embrace this innovation
I implore you one and all

To revolutionize the workplace
And to be proud of what we do.
Our nation will thank you in years to come
For the achievements of so few."

2025

The Development Application – Mosman

Trees already impede vision
Of views that I hold so dear
And with seniors blocking footpaths
I will lose my views, I fear

We all just want vibrant city living
And seniors don't belong
This development greatly concerns me
Can't they it's simply wrong?

There's the impact on our properties
With property prices devolving
But it's not about the money, trust me
There are principles involving

The worrying issue of building height
And the resulting loss of sunlight
Will lead to a shortage of Vitamin D
My posture must be tall and upright!

Can't they just live somewhere else
Somewhere where it doesn't matter?
Somewhere where they won't annoy us all
With their constant idle chatter?

Maybe assisted dying
Is the option now best suited
Do they really want to soldier on
in a world so crowded and polluted?

I'm sure they served our country well
But we can't dwell on the past in sorrow
We must think about the future!
We must focus on tomorrow!

I hear that's its nicer in the country
Where there's trees and other things
I read there's a need for population growth
In a place named Alice Springs

The old have so many options
And they really should not complain
And it's true that they constantly criticize
When they really should refrain

We must stop the proposed development
And make sure it is rejected
This aged care facility is ill-conceived
make sure that I'm elected!

2025

The Digital Childhood

My childhood was largely hidden
away from the public view
The joy and disappointments.
There were more than one or two

My trauma was deep and private
A very insular misery
Repercussions compounding
A confusing recovery

In the safe cocoon of grief recovering
One single step at a time
A gradual reawakening
A steady upward climb

In the lives of family and friends
some moments of joy were shared
an occasional photo in an album
But exposure certainly spared

My world was very little
like almost all humanity.
Overwhelmingly lives were lived
in relative obscurity

I hear of young entertainment celebrities
Who often transitioned badly
Into a deeply troubled adulthood
That often ended sadly

I was not the centre of attraction
in any exaggerated way
School, family, a small circle of friends
I just lived from day to day

I was not led to think I was exceptional
Little thought to what I might become
Safely stepping and occasionally stumbling
The once prerogative of the young

My life didn't span the stratosphere
It barely spanned my street!
I wasn't a junior influencer
the world wasn't at my feet

And today my digital profile
Is much less that it might be
I'm happy with a life lived rather well
Content in obscurity

But it's so different for many that I know
Those born in the digital age
Phones are the conduits of both good and bad

THE DIGITAL CHILDHOOD

In a most pervasive way

Each experience is digitalized
However great or small
And amplified across the planet
And seen by one and all

Now every child is a celebrity
exceptional and the best
With a significant online existence
in our post-modern affluent west

The task to create the perfect child
a frequent consuming quest
When parental oversight guarantees
success in every test

This digital existence
captured on-screen every morning
just as a reflection captured Narcissus.
(A timely old Greek warning!)

And when adulation and innocence
are one day painfully swept away
when a digital dagger strikes their vulnerable heart
on one unexpected day

When on the bus or in their room
a mocking comment is made
with surgical precision
In the most devasting way

Be it from envy or disapproval
Body shaming or jealousy
A magnifying glass will scrutinize
On-line for all to see

This fishbowl existence

in full view in every way
Can become a horrid nightmare
the experts warn and often say

And the darkest possible content
Will lay siege to their innocence
Who will be there to spare them
From this online wickedness

It will be hard to dismiss or eradicate
So I ask who will mentor and advise
in the parallel universe that they inhabit
where exist fools and some quite wise?

I hope my concerns are unjustified,
and like Lear with vision impaired
unable to see how things really are.
I just hope they're well prepared.

2025

The Wonderful Age Of Silence

The golden age of silence
has arrived so gradually
It started off so slowly
And rather hard to see

Of course, silence always existed
In our sleep and in our prayers
The monks of medieval times
Were removed from earthly cares

In those moments of quite solitude
They were the silent minority
They prayed for all humanity
To evoke heavenly authority

THE WONDERFUL AGE OF SILENCE

But now it's so much better
And I say without hesitation
In the crowded trains of suburbia
And on the platform whilst we're waiting

It's a 'tap on tap' off existence
No need to touch or converse
The risk of chat and germs is minimized
In our little universe

At the supermarket checkouts
Self-service is what we do
And you can steal a packet of razor blades
Or some toiletries or glue

The smart phones are our saviours
We need never be alone
These wonderful digital devices
Our hallowed mobile phone!

We can text our family members
As they spread through-out our mansions
In the labyrinths of the many rooms
Why have family interactions?

We can get rid of friends so easily
No need for face to face
No need to confront and talk it through
We're a consumer human race!

At the early morning school gates
The parents in numbers stand around
They are busily glued to their mobile phones
So close but not a sound

We can shop on-line so easily
For friends and romance too
In the modern way of dating

It's the easiest thing to do

And in this splendid isolation
of our solitary lives,
Is that loneliness I see upon your face or
perhaps a tear within your eye?

2025

The Rant

Just one day from the big election
and tempers are getting frayed
at the polling stations in marginal seats
It was in the news today

Social cohesion once was strong
And clever wit was celebrated with the
harmless banter at polling stations
with tension quite dilated

And the news reported yesterday
Of gross customer misbehaviour
Customers yelling abuse
In the supermarkets of Australia

Parents brawling at a soccer match
At an under-seven's game
Apparently, the fuse was lit when a goal was missed
Then came ridicule and blame

De-humanized women stare blankly
On a catwalk barely dressed
Enhancement to the point of dysmorphia
So sullen and acquiesced

Drug money and money laundering
Inflate the cost of real estate

THE RANT

Pushing up property prices
In every territory and state

School principals are not respected
With widespread bullying and intimidation
It makes me wonder what is going on
In the heartbeat of our nation

We're no longer noble citizens
Not proud of our culture and nation
We're a rag-tail bunch of sad consumers
Quite angry and frustrated

The social media algorithms
Confirm the simmering outrage
And the anger continues unabated
For those in a digital cage

Chatbots are sought by teenagers
For advice when they are upset
But the advice is the voice of an algorithm
With no care and no regret

Discourse at the dinner table
Is just a lingering memory
It's laptops and phones and dinner for one
In our fractured families

In just decades we've become so tribal
Our social contract much eroded
with family, faith and freedom
no longer cherished or upheld

Now critical race theory prevails
In our Post-Christian, Postmodern West
Nothing is objectively true these days
Should you put it to the test

'Men' and 'women' are disappearing
Will gender language remain?
We'll soon be 'seeding' or 'birthing' persons
Are we simply going insane?

We're told to feel guilty about our history
Those narratives of violence and of shame
It's those 'old age Western institutions'
That we denigrate and blame

And so, in this era of cultural suicide
as we devour our very selves
rabies infects the Western mind
For how long I cannot tell

And yet, I see so many shinning eyes
In the faces of those I teach
They give me hope for a better world,
A world just within our reach.

2025

Decolonisation

A letter arrived a few months ago
From the Department of Decolonisation
We opened it with trepidation
Because of our family situation

My wife was born in Italy
And came here as a child
Naturalisation followed as it normally does
Even though it took a while

I was born in England
And I too am naturalised
The contents of the letter
Brought tears to both our eyes

DECOLONISATION

Our citizenship has been revoked!
This can no longer be our home.
We are to make arrangements to leave Australia
So, I called them on my phone

A departmental officer explained politely
The process of decolonization
My wife and I would need to
Return to our birthplace nations

We would be given assisted passage
To help overcome the cost,
And our home would be bought at the market price
To minimize our loss

Our two sons would also have to leave
And they should complete some forms as well
They should both apply as a matter of haste
I increasingly felt unwell

But I downloaded all the applications
and sent them overseas
There was a contact in Italy and in England
To contact as I pleased

You can imagine my shock and horror
When we received a response my mail
Our applications were denied to us
Our applications had failed

Apparently, Italy and England are full
Because of overseas migration
I'm talking about the waves of humanity
Who have exhausted all accommodation

It seems as if Europe is being colonized
By young men from overseas
They arrive in inflatable dinghies

On tides with assisted breeze

The pubs of England are already full
Hostel options also gone
There's nowhere to stay it's sad to say
This surely is so wrong

But we were told we had other options
Where population growth is declining
A resettlement program was underway
And that every cloud has a silver lining

North Africa or Pakistan
Could be our home in months to come
If we sign on the line and return the form
We could resettle ahead of some

The world has gone wild and crazy
Who is going to accept the blame?
Decolonisation is gross lunacy
The world is increasingly insane.

2025

Character – Acts 10

Some waited in the public square
To catch up on the latest news
The Council of Jerusalem had just ended
This council of the Christian Jews

For days the debate had been heated
With passion and points debated
Whether to accept Cornelius
Who prayed and patiently waited

It certainly was a thorny question
Cornelius was neither Jew nor circumcised

CHARACTER – ACTS 10

He certainly couldn't speak Hebrew
He could speak Greek to just get by

Regarding Mosaic law he knew nothing
Yet he pleaded to be accepted
His sincerity and good character were not doubted
Still, some wanted him rejected

Peter and James conferred at length
Many hours late at night
To accept or reject the Centurion
To act wisely, just and right

They remembered the command of Jesus
To make disciples in all the nations
To convert the Greeks and the Philippians
As well as the Galatians

And what of sincerity and good character?
(The proclamation of just decades ago
Martin Luther King – "I have a dream!"
It's true, and sad I know,)

That good character is now devalued
As are the grand narratives of yesterday
They are rejected or undervalued
In the usual post-modern way

Now values are no longer objective
There's just a particular point of view
Nothing is absolute these days
Nothing is objectively true

Today 'character' is hardly here or there,
There's little that is right or wrong,
Moral relativism casts asunder,
As we move to a discordant song

Anyhow, Cornelius was accepted
Apparently, a decision correctly made
The means by which he was wisely judged,
remain valuable today.

2025

"But What Have The Romans Ever Done For Us?"

It's Roman day in England
Celebrations in the nation
Enactments in so many towns and schools
Recall the military invasion

Some dress up as Romans
And some as followers of Boudica
Mock fights are fought in schools and fields
With yelling, screams and cheer

It's the learning of old history
With feasting as in days of old
It's a day of much excitement
If the truth be fairly told

Britain has had waves of invasion
But the Romans are very special
Vikings and Normans almost equally so
In England they also settled

Waves of invasion are absorbed
The blood of invaders converges
To make the DNA of the country
As cultures and languages merge

Ireland does not celebrate Cromwell Day
It is still recovering from the pain

The living memory still lingers on
Split blood is a bitter stain

But most invaders offer something
That is valued when calmly viewed
As the voices of victims acquiesce
And on that I now conclude.

July 2025

I Wish I Was A Smart Phone

I wish I was a Smart Phone
Then I could catch my daddy's eye
He seems so absent from me
No matter how hard it is I try

I do a little dance
And I sing a little song
I just want some attention
Is what I wish so wrong?

I know dad is busy with work stuff
He has made that very clear
But I just wish that he would just look at me
His eyes I hold so dear

My mum also has a Smart Phone
And she too is often distracted
Even when I'm in the stroller
To the screen she is attracted

I'd like a bedtime story
When I go to my little bed
Because I get a little frightened
When there's monsters in my head

So, I shut my eyes and go to sleep

And dream of what might be
I dream of being a Smart Phone
With a screen for all to see.

June 2025

Toxic Town

Matthew 13:58

Their hearts are hardened, and their eyes are mocking
Yes, I struggle in this place
The town folk of my childhood
With so many a familiar face.

Imposter syndrome? Perhaps
But I don't think that's really true
It's the derision and rejection
Of more than just a few

"You were the carpenter's son
He made my family table,
He was skilled and very fair
Hardworking and very able

But you now claim to be a Messiah
Such a crazy weird idea!
I think you must have lost the plot
You've become delusional I fear"

My friends look so disheartened.
I see disappointment in their eyes
They don't criticize or malign me
They accept I failed but tried

So, I'll shake the dust off my sandals.
I must leave and go this day
There are still so many in need of healing

I will just continue on my way.

2025

Dads And Sons

Today I saw some dads and sons
at the doctor's surgery
One dad was rather young
With his new-born on his knee

Another dad was advanced in age
With a tube in his nose inserted
He was also obviously rather deaf
With his youth now quite deserted

And with him was his faithful son,
Concerned about food gone mouldy
But who spoke with real affection
To his dad now frail and oldly

The father son relationship
That holds them both together
The complementary profiles
The love that binds and tethers

The journey through the decades
The shift in dependency
The slowly shifting sand of time
That comes to you and me

Let's give thanks to all those dads and sons
who hold it all together,
In a thousand ways both big and small
May their love sustain forever.

2019

Hostile Dog

I went cycling this afternoon.
It was the perfect time to go.
The sun was shining the air was cool.
One of winter's finest shows.

And on my homeward journey
On this blissful cycling track
I approached a dog and owner
I approached them from their backs

The dog was off the leash
The leash in the owner's hand.
The dog was crouched on a patch of grass
For a toilet stop unplanned

I quietly cycled past them
The dog noticed and then gave chase
It was snarling as it approached my foot
So I accelerated with haste

I elevated my left leg
As it lunged to bite my skin
I accelerated just out of reach
I found the strength within

I called out over my shoulder
"Just keep it on a lead!"
Then I heard it yelping
Strong punishment indeed

I've had my share of family dogs
And I believe in proper training
Little treats and rewards will achieve
What is needed without straining

HOSTILE DOG

I warned some other people
On their way towards the dog
"There's a dog up ahead and I hope it's leashed
They gave me a thankful nod

A minute later I heard more growls
Another hostile confrontation
The snarling barking aggressive tone
A regrettable situation

And people are not so dis-similar
And If when young we are purposely brutalised
Aggression and beatings will guarantee
No hope of peace within our lives

It's the Middle East conundrum
Down the rabbit hole of hate.
To despise our fellow humans
I just hope it's not too late.

To see the stranger as a potential friend
And not a dangerous outsider
To celebrate what we have in common
And not the differences that divide us.

Like the dog that happily wags its tail
As it sees an approaching potential friend
Not a threat to its existence
With no hatred to transcend.

August 2025

"Proud sponsors of having a crack"

So NRL games to be held in Vegas?
A fantasy or is this true?
A few games will held in the USA
Come over and join in the queue

'Growing the sport in the USA'
This the call that is heard
(As if the game has a future in the USA
The idea is simply absurd!)

But there are untapped dollars in Vegas
With so many punters there to recruit
It's not about the actual game stupid!
The purpose is beyond dispute

You see, Americans are underperforming
When online betting is analysed
Just a fraction of our per capita spending
With opportunities to capitalise

The business model is compelling
The Excel spreadsheet tells no lies
The profits that can be made in the USA
The profits may stretch to the sky

The betting companies make millions
And funnel some of it back to the sport
Hospitals and schools are strapped for cash
Is there money for stadiums? Of course!

Horse racing exists just for betting
We all know this is obviously true
It's as boring as shit seeing a horse race around
Unless you're winning on horse number 2.

The confluence of passion and drinking

And 'having a bet with a mate'
(Linked to domestic violence increasing
We prefer not to have this debate)

But why not broaden the scope of the betting
And place bets on the players as well
As to who will suffer concussion, and in years to come,
Who will have brains that will turn into gel?

It's the best scheme for wealth redistribution
By sponsoring just "having a crack"
The flow of money from the poor to the very rich
With Buckley's chance of getting it back

A fool and his money are soon parted
Too easy it seems to be true
They won't get a buck from my wallet
Can I say the same for you?

16th October 2025

Profiling

Alarm expressed on the news tonight
Stop and search and Victorian law
A warrant is no longer needed
Concern for what's now in store

Concern regarding civil liberties
And erosion of our rights
This over-reach of law enforcement?
It was on the news tonight

Apparently First Nations people and Africans
attract the bulk of police attention
those from the Middle East are in 3rd place
the report went on to mention

But what about profiling based on age
Young, say about 40 years and under?
Do they attract the bulk of police attention?
I cannot help but wonder.

And then what about gender profiling?
Is it mostly men who are stopped when out?
Do women attract equal police attention?
An even gender split? I doubt

And then there's fashion profiling
Police watching those in hoodies
But maybe it's simply cold outside
And not a baddie but a goodie

By one means or by another
Profiling is here to stay
By fashion, race, age or by gender
It was on the news today.

Unpaired Words

Unpaired words are those words
Where the opposite does not exist
For example, there is no opposite
For the emphatic word 'desist'

Nike says "just do it"
Their slogan does not say, 'sist'
(Although 'desist' is used from time to time
When it's foolish to resist)

Well-dressed adults can be 'hevelled'
As they dine on food and wine
Dishevelled is the opposite
Like unkempt, it suggests decline

Whereas kempt is never said or heard
But it must mean looking good
Perhaps in a stylish suit of green
Like that worn by Robin Hood

Many will accept these vagaries
In the language that we speak
You are 'plussed' (and not 'nonplussed')
With no sense of feeling 'pique'

But if you are genuinely irritated
By how weird our language is
Write a letter to your tabloid
As a certified language whiz.

December 2025

I Want To Be A Bureaucrat

I want to be a bureaucrat
In a tall and shiny tower
Perhaps upon the 14th floor
In an office with a shower

I'd wear the burden of leadership
With a certain sense of pride
With talents and abilities
There's no real need to hide

I'd make some big decisions
In a very strategic way
And use the industry jargon
Whenever I have my say

I'd glow in the pride of achievement
Of progress and reform
There'd be targets, goals and working parties
These things will be the norm

The morning teas would be lavish
With platters of sandwiches and wraps
We all deserve a little indulgence
There's no real wrong in that!

Of course I'll make some errors
Some gigantic ones at that
But I'd sweep them under the carpet
There's a knack in doing that

We can hide behind each other
When the stuff hits the proverbial fan
Resist the urge to apologise
Obey the legal man!

If there is a mess that needs some action
From an error that has been made
There's always money that can be paid out
To make it go away

No accountability to speak of
No ICAC or ASIC to fear
No revelation of corruption
There's nothing to see here

There'd be a limit of reviews and feedback
And if the message was quite bad
It would just be a misunderstanding
No real lessons to be had

I'd filter from the organization
Those who question and ask why?
Trouble-makers and the doubters
They're such a waste of time

I'll promote a team of managers
But I'll call them leadership
I'll insist upon their loyalty

No need to 'rock the ship'

Psychopaths and narcissists
And yes, whilst they do persist,
In this worthy organisation
They simply don't exist!

2019

Vale Ann Marie Smith

Vale to Anne Marie Smith
You suffered out of sight
In a chair for a full 12 months
With no care and no respite

This callous disregard for life
No shred of love of care
Your body wasting by the day
Imprisoned In your chair

Six hours a day I've heard it said
Was your daily allocation
Of personal care just 1 to 1
A reasonable situation?

Yet this travesty of basic decency
Such an appalling disregard
Of basic human dignity
From those who should stand guard

Christ weeps to see your suffering
He touches your rotten flesh
He cries in consolation
As he holds you to his chest

Suffer the weak and disabled
Those without a voice

Those without an advocate
Those who have no choice

A daughter, friend and sister
A neighbour just next door
The silence of the suffering
Angels to the core

Advance Australia fair we sing
Let us all rejoice!
Are we really young and free I ask?
Some sadly have no choice.

2020

The Resurrection Strategic Plan [1]

The leaders of the sect conferred
To discuss a pressing problem
The committee members looked a little perplexed
In addressing their conundrum

"We need to give our church a boost
To re-ignite the flame
At the moment we're looking very tired
And just a little lame."

So they considered the need for a focus-group
That could confer and then submit
Some goals as part of a strategic plan
That would prove to be a hit

"We'll need to hire some consultants
For their expertise and vision
Because the stakes are high and between you and I

---
[1] My attempt to write a resurrections story in total contrast to that found in the New Testament

THE RESURRECTION STRATEGIC PLAN

We need to validate our mission

A delegate put his hand up slowly
He had the beginning of an idea
He spoke in trepidation
With a noticeable hint of fear

"If I may be permitted
To speak my point of view
I have an idea that just might work
That I'd like to share with you."

"We just need a resurrection story
To boost our hearts and minds
To assist both growth and renewal
And to share with all mankind

There was consternation immediately
A few spoke in opposition
"It's a very risky step to take
But given our situation"..

"Who would we claim to be resurrected?
What story would we tell?
The associated risk I have to say renders
me both dizzy and unwell!"

Another speaker raised his hand and spoke
"We can say we had always known
Of this resurrection story
But were heavenly instructed to reveal it now
And to reveal it in its glory"

To guide a special focus group
Some guidelines were formulated
They were hurriedly but carefully written down
In dot points and they stated:

That there should be a sample group
That we can expose this wild claim to
To test the water as we go, and if need
To adjust our point of view

That we will need convincing witnesses
Whose testimony until now unfounded
Whose witness statements will unequivocally
Render our followers amazed and quite astounded

That our approach will be softly-softly
To reduce the likelihood of resistance
We don't want to pay too high a price
So, we aim for acceptance not insistence

That our resurrection proclamation
Will involve a monument most sacred
With a ritual quite lavish in tone
It's importance can't be understated

That feedback would be ongoing
That we may pivot as we go
(Resurrection stories are a gamble
As most of you should know)
That the approach will be very corporate
(Though it must not seem as so
Our top-down strategies have had mixed success
as our track record clearly shows)

The meeting ended positively
The members did confidently express
That within a century or two the Resurrection Strategic Plan
could be a great success.

2025

The Good Bloke

He ticks all the necessary boxes
For being a decent sort of bloke
He'll go far in this organisation
He can tell a decent joke

He's not too smart or savvy
But steady as she goes
He stays away from controversy
He doesn't step on toes

He's not a polished public speaker
It's been noticed by some folk
He might stumble if a little nervous
This recognized 'good bloke'

His grades at uni. were average
never considered all that bright
Some have questioned his ascendancy
And wondered if it's right

He won't ask the tricky questions
Or say, "this surely is insane!"
He'll protect the organization
He knows the rules of the game

He'll nod his head and smile quite nicely
To those more senior than him
He won't ask the tricky question
He'll look knowingly or just grin.

He is referred to as a 'leader'
But if the truth was clearly told
He just a manager of the status quo
Compliant and not bold

He's a small target bureaucrat
Who tries never to offend
He won't nail his flag to any mast
So, he has little to defend

Reliable and predictable
And obsequious when required
In the beige landscape that he inhabits
There's next to no chance he will be fired

He's a bureaucratic square peg
On a board with nice square holes
He fits in so very nicely
If the truth be clearly told

He could our Prime Minister
He could really go that far
He's a dimly lit space traveller
Not a bright shining star

Don't ask him to be bold or visionary
They are traits he is without
But he's a mid-level good bloke man
Of that there is no doubt!

2020

The Quest For Chocolate Biscuits

My mother heard some quiet noises
In the middle of the night
She gave my dad a nudge to wake him
He awoke quickly and in fright

"I think I hear some movement Jock"
She whispered in his ear
"I hear noises from a room downstairs
It's the biscuit thief I fear"

So, my dad crept quietly down the stairs
Listening intently as he crept
The noises he followed guided him
To where the biscuits were always kept

Catherine had pleaded innocence
She was as honest as they came
And yet Stephen who still slept in a cot
Could hardly be to blame?

My dad approached the kitchen
No light shone below the door
In darkness he quietly went inside
He was stunned at what he saw

In the light from the kitchen window
He saw my shape very much suspended
I had climbed up the drawers of the kitchen dresser
To reach the biscuits undefended

And I must have leaned back in my surprise
My father could instantly see
The dresser tipping and starting to fall
To land heavily on me!

He ran toward the dresser

And shoved his shoulder against the wood
He grabbed me with his other arm
He saved me well and good

I was too young to recall this escapade
My memory has no recollection
It's in the memory archives of my family
My heartfelt gratitude I now mention.

December 2025

www.ingramcontent.com/pod-product-compliance
Lightning Source LLC
Chambersburg PA
CBHW071348080526
44587CB00017B/3016